"The path to recovery in anorexia is often confusing and convoluted. *The Anorexia Recovery Skills Workbook* provides a structured map for _____ ___ides hope and practical tools for recovery, while acknowledg_____ _____ overy process and giving permission for struggle. Clinicians ar_____ to be an integral part of treatment for this complex eating dis_____

—**Nicole Siegfried, PhD**, clinical director at The Highlands-Castlewood Treatment Centers

"This workbook is a practical and helpful tool for individuals working towards recovery from anorexia nervosa. The inspirational quotes, case examples, and ample opportunities for self-reflection make it user friendly and also quite personalized. I commend the authors for providing another, and much-needed, contribution to the tool kits of eating disorders treatment."

—**Ovidio Bermudez, MD**, chief clinical officer and medical director of child and adolescent services at the Eating Recovery Center

"*The Anorexia Recovery Skills Workbook* is a wise, compassionate, and comprehensive book! I just wish it had appeared on the shelves many years ago, so I could have used it when I was struggling. I highly recommend this book!"

—**Jenni Schaefer**, author of *Goodbye Ed, Hello Me* and coauthor of *Almost Anorexic* and *Life Without Ed*

The

Anorexia Recovery Skills
Workbook

A Comprehensive Guide to Cope with Difficult
Emotions, Embrace Self-Acceptance & Prevent Relapse

CATHERINE L. RUSCITTI, PsyD

JEFFREY E. BARNETT, PsyD, ABPP

REBECCA A. WAGNER, PhD

New Harbinger Publications, Inc.

Distributed in Canada by Raincoast Books

Copyright © 2017 by Catherine L. Ruscitti, Jeffrey E. Barnett, and Rebecca A. Wagner
        New Harbinger Publications, Inc.
        5674 Shattuck Avenue
        Oakland, CA 94609
        www.newharbinger.com

Cover design by Amy Shoup

Acquired by Elizabeth Hollis Hansen

Edited by Jennifer Eastman

Library of Congress Cataloging-in-Publication Data on file

19   18   17

10   9   8   7   6   5   4   3   2   1   First Printing

*To all of the brave women and men who have fought and
continue to fight for recovery from an eating disorder*

Contents

Foreword

Over the years, I have worked with many patients suffering from serious eating disorders. While we make great strides in treatment during our therapy sessions, I have often wished that I had a comprehensive, knowledgeable resource for patients to work with between our sessions. Furthermore, public health experts continue to remind us that only a fraction of patients struggling with diagnosable eating disorders will be able to access specialized eating disorder treatment. *The Anorexia Recovery Skills Workbook* fulfills this need to aid patients, families, and nonspecialized mental health professionals in accomplishing recovery from these serious illnesses. Although not intended as a self-help intervention to be used instead of close work with professional help, this informed, structured workbook can be an outstanding resource for *all* those working on recovery from an eating disorder.

This workbook has many strengths. Drs. Ruscitti, Barnett, and Wagner do an excellent job of reviewing what we know about the causes of eating disorders from a biopsychological perspective. This overview helps clarify that anorexia nervosa is a complex, lethal illness that usually requires multifaceted treatment delivered by an interdisciplinary team of professionals. The authors also offer a very helpful menu of questions that patients and families can use to assess the level of expertise of various team members.

The heart of the book deals with the psychological challenges of recovering from anorexia nervosa. Drs. Ruscitti, Barnett, and Wagner explain that they are drawing from the three most widely recognized psychotherapy strategies: cognitive behavioral therapy (CBT), dialectical behavior therapy (DBT), and acceptance and commitment therapy (ACT). Using all three of these formats, they identify clear treatment goals and exercises to help accomplish change. They also provide a sophisticated overview of the risks for relapse and make recommendations for minimizing these risks. Another important strength of this useful workbook is how the authors have expertly integrated cutting-edge research findings into all their recommendations and the activities they include to enhance the recovery process.

Overall, this workbook is an excellent tool to help patients and their families understand the illness of anorexia nervosa and the challenges of recovery. It is loaded with rating scales, checklists, questionnaires, exercises, and activities to promote recovery. Drs. Ruscitti, Barnett, and Wagner even had the thoughtful insight to include many of these tools online to cater to technology-savvy individuals. Each chapter begins with a clinical vignette that gives a real-world flavor to the points being made, and the language is understandable. Drs. Ruscitti, Barnett, and

Wagner have done a masterful job of translating complex biopsychosocial risk factors into everyday language and offering practical solutions to the problems posed by these factors. This workbook should be an outstanding resource to *any* person working on recovering from an eating disorder. Its use can easily be integrated into work with one's treatment team to promote and enhance the recovery process. I would recommend this book to any of my patients, not only for use during our treatment together, but as a resource that they can return to over and over again throughout their course of recovery.

> —Craig Johnson, PhD
> Chief Science Officer at the Eating Recovery Center
> Clinical Professor of Psychiatry at the University of the
> Oklahoma College of Medicine

Introduction

Welcome! You have made one of the most important decisions of your life: you have decided to recover from your eating disorder. You are likely feeling scared and nervous and hopeful and eager, all at the same time. This may seem to be a confusing response when committing to something so important, but it is normal. Choosing to recover from anorexia nervosa is the first of many steps you will take in recovery. Thinking about the steps that remain can seem overwhelming and exhausting; however, remember that recovery and living a meaningful life are worthwhile and rewarding.

Before jumping into the content of this book, it is important to discuss how to best use this book and to help determine if this is the right workbook for you! So take a deep breath and let's move forward in talking about anorexia nervosa, the process of recovery, and how this workbook can be an important and helpful resource to you as you work toward recovery.

Who Can Benefit from This Workbook?

This workbook was developed to be a resource for individuals in recovery from anorexia nervosa, to be used in conjunction with a psychotherapist. Because "recovery" is a personal and individually defined concept, further discussion of what it means to be "in recovery" is provided toward the end of this introduction. This book is based on research into the factors that contribute to maintaining recovery from anorexia rather than what is needed for someone just setting out on the road to recovery. Therefore, some of the skills, techniques, and concepts in this workbook apply primarily to individuals who are in a less structured setting, such as a partial hospitalization program or an intensive outpatient program. However, individuals in a more structured setting, like a residential treatment center, can also benefit from using this workbook, both in their current structured treatment setting and as they transition to lower levels of care. Additionally, while this book is based on research with adult women, the techniques and concepts can be generalized to the recovery process for men and older adolescents with anorexia as well.

How Do I Use This Workbook?

This workbook uses guided readings to help you understand more about yourself and your environment. It is designed for you to learn from others and help you find solutions to barriers that keep you from achieving your goal of recovery. It is best used along with outpatient psychotherapy. While it can be a tool you use on your own in your recovery process, research suggests that the therapeutic use of books is most effective when a psychotherapist is involved in the treatment (Mains and Scogin 2003). Using this book along with psychotherapy can help focus treatment and bring awareness to issues that may arise as you work through the recovery process. For these reasons, this workbook will present information with the assumption that you are receiving care from a psychotherapist, and it will often suggest that you discuss and work on specific ideas or exercises with members of your treatment team.

Why Is This Workbook Important?

Each chapter of this workbook focuses on a theme that research has shown to be important in fostering and maintaining recovery from anorexia (Federici and Kaplan 2008; Granek 2007; McFarlane, Olmsted, and Trottier 2008; Nilsson and Hagglof 2006; Patching and Lawler 2009; Tozzi et al. 2003; Vanderlinden et al. 2007). These factors include

- managing difficulties that can arise after inpatient treatment is completed and maintaining the progress that has been made;

- creating and maintaining a treatment team;

- rebuilding healthy relationships and decreasing unhealthy relationship patterns;

- developing an understanding of your eating disorder;

- gaining a sense of independence;

- giving up control of your eating disorder and regaining control in healthier aspects of your life;

- developing more positive feelings about yourself and your life outside of your eating disorder—and about your weight and body size.

- improving your self-acceptance and self-efficacy, which will facilitate and maintain internal motivation to recover;

- developing healthy goals for yourself, including both goals related to healthy eating and goals unrelated to your eating disorder, such as career, academic, and recreational goals that will assist you to lead a fulfilling life;

- taking time to practice self-care;

- planning and preparing yourself for challenging and difficult times throughout recovery; and

- maintaining changes in behavior and thought patterns, such as awareness and tolerance of negative emotions, reaching out for help when needed, and effective communication.

What Can I Expect from This Workbook?

This workbook provides evidence-based information and tools to help you identify issues you may be facing currently or may eventually face in the recovery process. It also will assist you in finding support and encouragement to continue on the path of recovery and to properly care for your own well-being during recovery. As you proceed through this workbook, there are a few things you should keep in mind:

- The chapters do not need to be read in a particular order and are designed to be revisited as needed throughout your recovery.

- The terms *anorexia*, *anorexia nervosa*, and *eating disorder* are used interchangeably throughout; but the information in the book is based in research and is tailored specifically for those in recovery from anorexia, not from eating disorders in general.

- Each chapter provides an overview of the importance of a particular theme, as well as tools, coping skills, strategies, and suggestions to help you to participate more fully and effectively in your recovery process.

- Rating scales, checklists, questionnaires, exercises, and activities are included to help you apply the information to your own life and practice the skills described in each chapter.

- Many of the exercises and worksheets are also available at http://www.newharbinger .com/39348.

The therapeutic concepts, skills, and techniques described in this workbook come from three main types of therapy: cognitive behavioral therapy (CBT), dialectical behavior therapy (DBT), and acceptance and commitment therapy (ACT). These are evidence-based and widely used approaches to treating eating disorders (Bankoff et al. 2012; Galsworthy-Francis and Allan 2014; Sandoz, Wilson, and DuFrene 2010). CBT focuses on how thoughts and behaviors impact our emotions; it emphasizes changing thought patterns and behaviors as a way of altering emotion states (Beck 2011). DBT and ACT stem from CBT but differ in several ways. DBT focuses on the balance of acceptance and change and emphasizes skills related to tolerating distress, improving interpersonal communication and relationships, regulating emotions, and engaging in mindfulness (Linehan 1993). ACT, on the other hand, focuses on accepting our internal experiences and creating distance from our thoughts and emphasizes using our values to guide our actions (Hayes, Stroshal, and Wilson 2012). Skills from each of these therapies are presented to help you address the topics in each chapter. The goal is for you to try out different skills and determine which are most helpful for you and your recovery.

Case examples are presented at the beginning of each chapter to illustrate how others might be impacted by and respond to the struggles and challenges of recovery. They will help you understand the concepts presented and will ensure that you have realistic expectations of yourself in the recovery process—and they also show that you are not alone. Each chapter ends with journaling pages; you may use them for your own self-reflection in order to process the information provided, as well as your reactions, feelings, and personal experiences related to each section. You may also find it useful to discuss what you write there with your psychotherapist, to serve as a starting place for in-depth discussions regarding your challenges, struggles, and successes in recovery.

It is important to note that this workbook does not replace or reduce the importance of maintaining and utilizing a therapeutic treatment team as you go through recovery and work to prevent relapse. Instead, it should actively be used along with psychotherapy to add to it and enhance it. By implementing the readings and exercises from this workbook between sessions, you can explore any difficulties you have in recovery both in and out of session, enhancing the therapeutic process.

Now that the specifics of this workbook have been introduced and explained, let's take some time to set the groundwork for the chapters that follow with a brief overview of anorexia and the recovery process.

What Is Anorexia Nervosa?

Eating disorders, such as anorexia nervosa, bulimia nervosa, binge-eating disorder, and other specified feeding or eating disorder, are mental illnesses that affect individuals psychologically, emotionally, physically, and interpersonally. As described in the mental health profession's diagnostic manual, the *Diagnostic and Statistical Manual of Mental Disorders* (DSM-5), anorexia nervosa is characterized by a restriction of caloric intake leading to significantly low body weight for one's age, sex, developmental trajectory, and physical health; a distorted body image or lack of recognition of the seriousness of one's low body weight; and a significant fear of gaining weight or persistent behavior that inhibits weight gain (American Psychiatric Association 2013).

There are two main subtypes of anorexia that may be experienced: restricting type and binge-eating-purging type. In the restricting type of anorexia nervosa, a patient limits caloric intake or exercises excessively but has not regularly engaged in binge-eating or purging behavior, such as self-induced vomiting or the misuse of laxatives, diuretics, or enemas. On the other hand, in binge-eating-purging type, the patient has regularly engaged in binge-eating or purging behaviors (e.g., self-induced vomiting, laxative use, overexercising) over the past three months (American Psychiatric Association 2013). Anorexia nervosa affects approximately 0.9 percent of females and 0.3 percent of males in the United States (Hudson et al. 2007). They often have difficulty maintaining interpersonal relationships. In addition, they often experience depression, anxiety, and obsessive-compulsive symptoms; frequently lack a healthy sense of identity; and often crave a sense of control (American Psychiatric Association 2013).

Anorexia nervosa has numerous dangerous health consequences, including cardiac problems, an intolerance to cold, the erosion of dental enamel, and osteoporosis (a loss of bone density). Death also can occur, either from severe physical complications or from suicide. In fact, anorexia nervosa is the deadliest of all mental illnesses (Arcelus et al. 2011; Sullivan 1995). Up to 20 percent of individuals suffering from anorexia will die from complications related to their eating disorder, and females between the ages of fifteen and twenty-four with anorexia are twelve times more likely to die from complications of their eating disorder than from any other cause (Crow, Praus, and Thuras 1999; Herzog et al. 2000; Sullivan 1995). Given the seriousness of anorexia, actively engaging in the recovery process is of great importance.

A range of treatment options is available for those suffering from anorexia nervosa. The type of treatment can vary based on the severity of one's illness, with treatment options including highly structured inpatient hospitalization, residential treatment facilities, partial hospitalization programs, intensive outpatient programs, and outpatient treatment. Within each setting, individuals typically work with a team of professionals, such as psychiatrists, individual psychotherapists, dietitians, group therapists, and family therapists. With treatment, it is estimated that nearly half of all individuals will achieve full recovery, approximately a third will remain symptomatic but demonstrate improvement, and about 20 percent remain chronically ill (Crow, Praus, and Thuras 1999; Herzog et al. 2000; Sullivan 1995). How actively each patient engages in the recovery process can significantly impact these results.

What Is Recovery?

Both professionals and individuals who are in recovery have a range of views on what constitutes a relapse and what criteria need to be met to be considered "in recovery" (Couturier and Lock 2006; Darcy et al. 2010). It is up to you and your treatment team to define what being in recovery means for you. While recovery is a personal experience, it is important to be aware of the inaccurate tendency to view recovery in an all-or-nothing way: *Either I'm "recovered" or I'm "eating disordered."* Regardless of your definition, recovery is an ongoing process with many ups and downs. It is something that you will need to actively work on, especially in the beginning, in order to prevent a relapse.

In this book, we will be using the phrase "in recovery" to describe someone who is actively engaged in the process of working toward both mental and physical health. This means you are committed to achieving and maintaining a healthy weight; you are committed to refraining from using eating disordered behaviors; and you are committed to living a meaningful life without your eating disorder. It is important to emphasize that being in recovery does not mean you will never slip up, experience bad days, or make mistakes from time to time. It does mean, however, that you are willing to be accountable for these lapses and recommit to moving forward toward better health.

Welcome!

Before we begin, we want to take a moment to welcome you to this process of recovery. We commend you for taking this important first step. This is likely going to be a tough process, as you take steps in your journey toward physical, mental, and emotional well-being, but it will be worthwhile. By committing to the recovery process, you have already taken a huge step. Now, let's take the next step and begin working through this workbook.

Chapter 1

Understanding the Process of Change

A journey of a thousand miles begins with a single step.

—Lao Tzu

Meet Mila

Mila has struggled with body image and disrupted eating patterns for years. She has not yet suffered any medical complications from her anorexia, but she fears that if she continues restricting her eating, she might damage her body. She is withdrawn from friends and family. Several people have commented on how thin she looks, but Mila does not think that she is thin enough. She feels in control when restricting her eating, and her ability to go long periods of time without eating makes her feel special. Despite receiving treatment in the past, Mila is still not sure that she has a problem. She is hesitant to change her behavior and is ambivalent about seeking future treatment. Even if she does decide to enter treatment, she worries about what treatment will entail this time, what her life will be like without the eating disorder and body image concerns, and if she will be able to sustain lasting recovery.

Like Mila, many people struggle with knowing whether they have a problem with eating and what to do about it. As you begin this workbook, an important first step is to evaluate if you have an eating disorder by answering a brief set of questions. Next, we will look at your motivation to change by examining the stages that people go through when making changes in their life. This section includes an exercise that will help you better understand your readiness for change. Knowing this will help you as you begin to think about treatment. However, before we talk about treatment, it is important to define what recovery looks like for you. Each person has different goals for treatment, so knowing these at the onset will help to shape what treatment looks like for you. The final section of this chapter explores available levels of treatment and explains how to use this information as you move forward in the workbook. We hope that this chapter will set a foundation for understanding yourself and your eating disorder that you can build on in subsequent chapters. Taking this first step can be scary, but we are here to guide you through this process.

Evaluating Where You Are in Your Eating Disorder

Before we jump into this workbook, it is a good idea to get a sense of where you are in your eating disorder and recovery. This assessment tool is designed to help you better understand your eating disorder symptoms and their severity. It gives you information about your behaviors and attitudes related to eating and body image, and it helps you determine areas in which you might be struggling. This list is not exhaustive, and there may be additional behaviors and attitudes that have impacted or continue to impact your eating disorder and recovery. There is space where you can add those ideas at the end. Remember that there are no right or wrong answers, so please take your time and be honest in answering the questions by indicating if each item is something you previously struggled with (Yes–Past), currently struggle with (Yes–Present), or if the item has not been applicable to your eating disorder and recovery (No). Your candid responses are an important first step in your recovery process.

	Yes–Past	Yes–Present	No
1. Are you restricting food by limiting calories, skipping meals, or cutting out food groups in a way that has led to low body weight?			
2. Do you have an intense fear of gaining weight or becoming fat?			
3. Do you struggle to recognize the seriousness of your low body weight?			
4. Do you binge eat (e.g., eating, within a discrete period of time, an amount of food that is larger than most people would eat under similar circumstances)?			
5. Do you feel a lack of control over your eating?			
6. Do you eat more rapidly than normal?			
7. Do you eat until you are uncomfortably full?			
8. Do you eat large amounts of food when not feeling physically hungry?			
9. Do you eat alone because you feel embarrassed by how much you are eating?			
10. Do you feel disgusted with yourself, depressed, or very guilty after eating?			
11. Do you engage in inappropriate compensatory behaviors after eating to prevent weight gain, such as vomiting, fasting, excessive exercise, or misuse of laxatives, diuretics, or other medications?			
12. Does the binge eating or use of inappropriate compensatory behaviors average at least once a week for the last three months?			
13. Do you have a significantly different view of your body shape and size than others have of you?			
14. Does how you feel about your body negatively affect how you see yourself?			
15. Do you feel distressed by your pattern of eating?			

If you answered Yes–Present to three or more of the above questions, you may be actively struggling with an eating disorder and treatment may be warranted. If most of your yes responses are in the Yes–Past column, it is likely that you have begun your journey to recovering from your eating disorder. Either way, if you are not already in treatment, we encourage you to consider seeking treatment. The next step—a simple one—is to assess your motivation to change, and after that we can look at what recovery means to you and explore the levels of available treatment.

Determining Motivation for Change

Change is difficult for most people. Deciding to make a change is a tough decision, but making and sustaining the change can be even more difficult. When deciding to change a behavior, like our pattern of eating, we go through various stages (Prochaska and Velicer 1997). The typical order you may progress through is described below. When changing behavior, many people relapse and return to an earlier stage several times before they achieve their goals. Each time this happens, they gain new information and will be able to apply that information to their next attempt.

Stages of Change

Precontemplation. During this stage, you do not believe that you have a problem and do not want to make changes. You may be aware of some of the consequences of the behavior but do not see them as a big deal in your life at present. Often you resist action-oriented interventions and advice on how to give up the behavior, but you may be open to information about risks and how to avoid or minimize them. As illustrated in the case example, Mila is unsure that she has a problem and is hesitant to seek treatment or change her behavior. Even though she has not experienced any physical problems so far, Mila is open to learning about the medical complications of eating disorders and how her behaviors will ultimately affect her well-being.

Contemplation. You begin to evaluate your use of restricting food intake and start to consider change. You are ambivalent about change and assess the advantages and disadvantages of the behavior. You might think to yourself: *I should give up the behavior, because of all the problems it's causing me, but what am I going to do instead? I'll miss it.* As Mila moves toward contemplation, she wants to consider the pros and cons of her restricting. The behavior serves a function for her (it makes her feel in control), but there are also unwanted side effects to contemplate (it isolates her from family and friends and impacts her health).

Determination and Preparation. This is the stage when you have decided that change is worthwhile, have made up your mind to cut down or quit restricting, and have begun to think about strategies to help you change. This is a planning stage, in which you set goals and identify internal and external supports and resources that can help you in making changes. During this stage, Mila is determined to stop restricting and may start researching treatment options.

Action. During this stage, you begin cutting down or stopping restricting behaviors. Support and skills training is part of this stage. Given how difficult it is to change these behaviors, it is important that you review the reasons that led you to the decision to make the change. At this stage, Mila has entered into treatment and is learning new skills to help her stop restricting. In meetings with her psychotherapist, she reviews the list of pros and cons she created when contemplating treatment to reinforce her decision to enter treatment.

Maintenance. Congratulations! You have made changes in your eating disorder behaviors and are sustaining them over time. Changes in behavior that are maintained for six months or more are often associated with substantial improvements in quality of life—in your relationships, physical and mental well-being, and employment. Without such improvements, the effort to change may not seem worth it, and relapse is more likely. It is recommended that you talk about the positive reasons for maintaining change in order to reinforce your decision and your efforts in making the change. Mila has been in treatment for six months and has stopped restricting. She is following her prescribed meal plan, exercising an appropriate amount, and continuing to address any struggles that arise during her therapy sessions. She feels good about her progress, sees improvements in her level of energy and ability to concentrate, and feels more connected in her relationships with others.

Relapse. At this stage, you return to eating disorder behaviors after a period of decreased use or no use. Relapse is viewed as a minor slip and is a normal part of the change process. Relapse is common and can be a onetime incident, but it may lead to regular use of the old behavior, which is why it is important that you see it as a learning experience. During a relapse, reassess your motivation for change and develop strategies to overcome the issues that contributed to the relapse. For Mila, she had been engaged in treatment and was starting to make changes in her restricting behavior but relapsed following a series of fights with her parents. It is important that Mila acknowledge the reemergence of her restricting, work with her psychotherapist to examine what happened during the fights, and identify healthier coping skills to use next time. It will also be important that she renew her drive to live a healthier life and get back on track with her meal plan.

Evaluate Your Motivation for Treatment

We have just reviewed the stages people go through when they are making changes in their life. Now, we'd like for you to take some time to explore where you are regarding your motivation for change. On the next page is a set of questions to help you better understand your readiness for change.

What stage of change are you currently in regarding your eating disorder, and what are the indicators that this is the stage you are in?

_____

_____

How important is it to you right now to change your eating disorder behavior?

_____

_____

What would have to happen to make it more important?

_____

_____

If you decided to change, how confident are you that you would succeed?

_____

_____

What would have to happen to make you more confident?

_____

_____

What barriers do you anticipate when making changes to your eating disorder?

_____

_____

What would have to happen to eliminate some of these barriers?

_____

_____

How ready are you to change?

_____

_____

How ready are you to commit to doing the work involved in being in recovery from your eating disorder?

_____

_____

_____

What would have to happen to make you more ready or committed?

_____

_____

_____

There are no right or wrong answers to the above questions; they are meant to help you evaluate where you are in the process of change. It is important to reflect on your answers to these questions. Did you identify anything that will make changing your eating disorder behavior more important or make you feel more confident about change? Did you think of any barriers that could get in your way or things that will make you more ready for change? If so, we encourage you to discuss these with your psychotherapist so you can begin to work through these challenges.

Defining Recovery

As mentioned in the introduction, it is important to define what recovery means for you. Recovery is different for everyone, as Angie and Kayla demonstrate:

Angie: *For me, recovery means that I'm actively working toward my goals. I'm following my meal plan and abstaining from unhealthy behaviors—purging, overexercising, counting calories, and weighing myself.*

Kayla: *What recovery means to me is that I'm staying out of intensive treatment by working with my outpatient team to maintain a healthy weight and reduce my behaviors like restricting, calorie counting, and using laxatives. I know recovery isn't perfect, so I accept slipups, but I will know that I'm still in recovery if I'm able to be honest about these slipups and can actively choose to continue toward my goals.*

Now take some time to reflect on your own recovery. What does recovery look like for you? What are some signs that may indicate you are in recovery? Write your ideas about this below. It may be helpful to share your responses with your psychotherapist to begin discussing expectations for recovery and how she or he may help you in achieving your goals.

_____

_____

_____

_____

_____

_____

_____

Levels of Care

When recovering from an eating disorder, there are various levels of treatment to consider. Let's look at the types of care available, and then we can examine how to determine which level of care is best for you.

Inpatient Hospitalization

The most intensive level of care you can participate in is inpatient hospitalization (IP). At this level of care, you are monitored in a hospital setting twenty-four hours a day because of medical complications related to your eating disorder. The length of stay at this level varies from several hours to several weeks, depending on how long it takes to get you medically stabilized. Typically, admission to this level of care means you have an acute physical or mental health risk and need close supervision.

Residential Treatment

A residential treatment facility offers extended care in a highly structured environment providing support twenty-four hours per day. It integrates a variety of therapy modalities throughout the day, such as individual psychotherapy, group therapy, nutritional counseling, medical monitoring, and alternative and complementary therapies. Length of stay varies from several weeks to several months depending on your ongoing treatment needs.

Partial Hospitalization

Partial hospitalization programs (PHP) provide patients with structured and supervised treatment for four to twelve hours per day, five to seven days per week, but patients return home each evening. It integrates a variety of treatment modalities, similar to those implemented in a residential treatment facility. By returning home each evening, this level of care offers you more freedom and responsibility to practice recovery on your own, an important step in the recovery process. The semi-structured level of care also costs less than residential programs. Length of treatment at this level of care varies from several weeks to several months.

Intensive Outpatient and Outpatient

The level of care received at an outpatient level can vary. Intensive outpatient (IOP) care provides you with structured and supportive care, including meal support and individual and group psychotherapy, several days per week. Outpatient (OP) care involves treatment and collaboration with a variety of providers, such as psychotherapists, dietitians, psychiatrists, and physicians. Once you are in OP, you typically meet with one or more treatment providers one to three times per week.

Guidelines Used to Determine Level of Care

Now that you know the levels of care available for treating an eating disorder, use the table on the next page to help you determine the best level of care for you based on your medical status, psychiatric status, motivation to recover, level of engagement and cooperativeness with treatment, response to treatment, need for supervision at meals, and degree of active eating disorder behaviors. Of course, this information should not replace the opinion and guidance of a professional, and we encourage you to seek consultation with a treatment provider to help you determine what level of care is most appropriate for you and your needs.

	Inpatient	Residential	Partial Hospital	IOP or OP
Medical Status	Unstable—a low heart or respiratory rate, low blood pressure, abnormal labs, complications from coexisting medical problems like diabetes or kidney dysfunction	Stable—no need for daily medical monitoring	Stable	Stable
Psychiatric Status	Unstable—rapidly worsening symptoms of anxiety, depression, mood instability, or suicidality	Impaired—severe symptoms of anxiety, depression, or mood instability	Stable	Stable
Motivation to Recover	Very poor to poor	Poor to fair	Fair	Fair to good
Level of Engagement or Cooperativeness in Treatment	Uncooperative or only cooperative in a highly structured environment	Only cooperative in a highly structured environment	Cooperative	Cooperative

Response to Treatment	Unable to respond to other lower levels of care	Unable to respond to partial hospitalization or outpatient treatments	Unable to respond to IOP or OP levels of care	Good
Need for Supervision at Meals	Yes	Yes	Some supervision and structure needed	Some to none needed
Degree of Active Engagement in Eating Disorder Behaviors	Active eating disorder behaviors	Active eating disorder behaviors	Active eating disorder behaviors	Mild to no active eating disorder behaviors

How Is This Insight Useful to Me?

Hopefully the information in this chapter has helped you better understand where you are in the process of your eating disorder and has provided you with guidance on possible treatment options. No matter where you are in your disorder, as you proceed through the workbook, we encourage you to complete the self-evaluation questions and use the information gathered as a way to direct your continued process of recovery.

This workbook can be helpful to people at any stage of recovery. As your illness improves, you will likely find yourself revisiting topics you've already covered. This is the normal cycle of recovery. Each time you explore a theme previously addressed in treatment, you have the opportunity to learn something new. It is unlikely that you are addressing the matter from the exact same perspective and under the same circumstances. Therefore, you may discover insight you had not previously considered.

If you already completed this workbook at an earlier phase of your recovery, we recommend that you complete the workbook again and see if your responses have changed. Each time you are exposed to the material here, you may deepen your understanding of your illness and discover new ways of using the concepts presented. The repetition involved in this process allows for greater reflection on your recovery journey and can help you measure progress over time.

Journaling Pages

In this chapter, we met Mila, who, like many people, does not know whether her pattern of eating is disordered. We hope that as you answered the questions in this chapter, you gained a better sense of whether your pattern of eating is problematic. We also looked at your motivation for and readiness for change. Finally, we clarified what recovery looks like for you and what levels of treatment are available, based on your treatment needs.

Before going on to the next chapter, take a moment to reflect on the concepts from this chapter. As you worked through the exercises, did you discover anything about yourself that surprised you? Maybe you are more or less willing or ready to change than you thought. Perhaps you had not considered what your goals for recovery are, and you found out that you really don't know what you want recovery to look like. Below, note these things, plus anything you have questions about or would like to discuss further with your treatment team.

_____

_____

_____

_____

_____

_____

_____

_____

_____

_____

_____

_____

_____

Chapter 2

Building Your Treatment Team

Alone we can do so little; together we can do so much.

—Helen Keller

Meet Destiny

Destiny recently stepped down to outpatient treatment after insurance declined further payment for her to be at a partial hospitalization program. She was given referrals from her partial program and has set up appointments to meet with a new psychiatrist and psychotherapist in the upcoming week. She is unable to afford a dietitian, and she is concerned about her ability to pay for her psychotherapist, who is out of network with her insurance. She hopes to discuss her payment options prior to her first appointment. However, she is struggling to accept that she needs to continue with so many appointments, because she believes she has made enough progress. She has restored her weight, her lab results are stable, and she has not used eating disordered behaviors since beginning intensive treatment. She knows that she needs to continue working on her relationships, communication with her family, and coping with her depression, but she also wants to take a brief break from treatment. She is determined to give outpatient treatment a try, but she is hesitant and skeptical that it is completely necessary at this time.

Because of the complex nature of anorexia nervosa, an interdisciplinary approach is often considered ideal in treating this disorder. This means that professionals from a variety of disciplines are involved in your case. Within inpatient, residential, and partial hospitalization programs, all the specialists who are necessary for you to make progress toward recovery are present and integrated into your treatment program—a primary care physician, psychiatrist, individual psychotherapist, family therapist, group therapist, and dietitian. Based on your needs, other members of your team may include an art therapist, movement therapist, yoga instructor, or psychodrama therapist. In outpatient care, you may utilize any combination of these specialists to create a treatment team, with a physician, psychiatrist, psychotherapist, and dietitian being the core members. For example, Destiny's partial hospitalization providers recommended outpatient treatment with a psychotherapist, psychiatrist, and dietitian. Because most structured programs (e.g., inpatient, residential, and partial hospitalization) integrate all of the necessary treatment team members into their programs, this chapter will focus on building your outpatient treatment team—which may stand alone or may be in addition to an intensive outpatient program—as this often requires using multiple resources and facilities.

As Destiny's case illustrates, creating an outpatient treatment team is just one part of the process. If you have been in more intensive treatment like Destiny, you may face similar issues—you may question what continued outpatient treatment you need, you may want to take a break from treatment after you leave an intensive program, and you might be ambivalent about just how much assistance you need in the recovery process. As we discuss these types of issues throughout the chapter, it is important to remember that recovery is an actual phase of the overall treatment process rather than something that happens automatically after a stint in intensive treatment. You must actively engage in the recovery process and do so with the appropriate team to have a good chance of success.

Creating Your Treatment Team

Research demonstrates that maintaining an outpatient treatment team is important for maintaining recovery from anorexia (e.g., Federici and Kaplan 2008). Outpatient treatment requires an interdisciplinary approach and, ideally, coordination and communication about your progress between your providers. Most often, you are responsible for initiating care from each of the necessary professionals and creating your own outpatient team. However, once you initiate contact with one provider, he or she may be able to give you recommendations or referrals regarding whom to contact to complete your treatment team. For example, your psychotherapist might give you names of reputable dietitians. This can help to reduce the amount of work you need to do. There is a variety of outpatient team members whom you should consider, but ideally all four of the specialists discussed below will be integrated into your team. In addition to these four, you might also consider others, such as an art therapist or movement therapist. Your psychotherapist can help you determine if additional team members like these might be helpful.

Psychotherapist

The role of your individual psychotherapist is to help you decrease eating disorder symptoms and deal with underlying issues that cause and maintain eating disordered thoughts and behaviors. Your psychotherapist will help you throughout your recovery to develop healthy coping skills to replace your reliance on your eating disorder. While individual therapy is the most common type of psychotherapy sought out by those with eating disorders, group therapy and family therapy are also available. There are three main types of psychotherapist you can consider. Below are brief descriptions of each:

Clinical or Counseling Psychologist—A psychotherapist who has completed approximately five years of graduate education in psychology. Psychologists also complete supervised clinical work prior to earning their degree. In some states, they are also required to complete one to two years of supervised clinical work after they earn their degree in order to be licensed. Psychologists typically have either a doctor of philosophy (PhD) or a doctor of psychology (PsyD) degree.

Counselor—A psychotherapist who has completed approximately two years of graduate education in psychology or counseling. Additionally, a counselor completes approximately two years of supervised clinical work before he or she can be licensed. Counselors typically have either a master of arts (MA) or a master of science (MS) degree.

Clinical Social Worker—A psychotherapist who has completed approximately two years of graduate education in social work. Like a counselor, a clinical social worker completes approximately two years of supervised clinical work before he or she can be licensed. Social workers typically have a master of social work (MSW) degree.

Regardless of the type of psychotherapist you choose, there are several important factors to consider. First, be sure that your clinician is licensed or supervised by someone who is licensed. Second, regardless of their degree or profession, if possible, choose a psychotherapist who has training and experience in working with individuals with eating disorders. Often, psychotherapists who specialize in eating disorders will have completed extensive supervised clinical experience in a treatment setting focusing on these disorders, such as an inpatient or residential program. It is important to make sure any psychotherapist you work with is well trained to work with you and address your treatment needs (on the following page, we list some questions you can ask that will help you determine this). Lastly, choose someone who is a good fit for you. Ask any questions or voice any concerns you may have during your initial meeting with your psychotherapist. It is important to find a psychotherapist whom you trust and with whom you feel comfortable. Remember that not every psychotherapist is going to be a good fit for you, so don't give up if the first one you meet does not work out. To help you find the right psychotherapist, on the following pages are some questions that can be helpful to ask either by phone or in your first visit. There are many things you want to consider when choosing a psychotherapist, so use this list of questions as a starting point. You may want to make copies of these questions so you can write down the responses from each psychotherapist you interview; this questionnaire is available at http://www.newharbinger.com/39348.

What is your experience and training (e.g., as a psychiatrist, psychologist, licensed counselor, social worker)?

_____

What is your experience in working with individuals in recovery from eating disorders?

_____

What is your approach to psychotherapy? What type of psychotherapy do you practice (e.g., cognitive behavioral therapy (CBT), dialectical behavior therapy (DBT), acceptance and commitment therapy (ACT)?

_____

_____

What do you believe are the best ways to treat eating disorders?

_____

_____

Do you treat individuals with comorbid disorders (e.g., other disorders that often accompany an eating disorder, such as anxiety, depression, bipolar, substance use, and personality disorders)?

_____

_____

Besides individual psychotherapy, what other types of psychotherapy do you provide (e.g., group therapy, workshops)?

_____

_____

I am also working with a dietitian, physician, and psychiatrist. How do you plan to coordinate care with them?

_____

_____

Can I engage in outpatient therapy with you if I am still struggling with eating disordered behaviors (e.g., restricting, bingeing, purging)?

_____

_____

What can I expect during sessions?

_____

_____

How involved is my family or significant other required to be? What do you believe is best in terms of including my family or significant other in my treatment?

_____

_____

How often will we meet? _____

What days and hours do you have available?

_____

How quickly can we schedule an initial appointment? _____

What are your financial policies? _____

_____

Do you accept insurance? _____

- What insurance do you accept? _____
- Is there a fee for missed appointments? _____
- How far in advance do I have to cancel to avoid a charge? _____
- Am I required to pay at each session? _____
- What forms of payment do you accept? _____

Are you available to talk by phone or e-mail? Is there a charge for this?

_____

Are you available for—and how do you respond to—crises and emergency situations?

_____

If I begin to relapse, how will you handle this? What types of difficulties will warrant a higher level of care for me?

_____

_____

Do you think we are a good fit? Would you like to work with me?

_____

Registered Dietitian or Nutritionist

The role of your dietitian or nutritionist is to provide nutritional counseling, stabilize and monitor your eating patterns and weight, and help with meal planning. Your dietitian or nutritionist will also monitor progress and potential symptoms of relapse as you proceed through recovery. A registered dietitian (RD) is someone who has a bachelor's or master's degree in nutrition and dietetics and who has completed supervised clinical training prior to being licensed. *Nutritionist*, on the other hand, is a nonaccredited title that does not require a degree in nutrition. Because the title *nutritionist* is not protected by law, individuals practicing under this title have widely varying levels of knowledge and experience. Therefore, it is important to inquire about the education and experience of a nutritionist. Also, as with your psychotherapist, it would be beneficial to choose a dietitian or nutritionist who has training and experience with individuals with eating disorders.

Psychiatrist

A psychiatrist is a physician (MD or DO) who has specialized postgraduate training in mental health treatment, typically focusing on treatment with medication. The role of your psychiatrist is to provide any medication needed throughout treatment. Your psychiatrist can prescribe and monitor medications that help stabilize your mood, decrease your anxiety, or lessen your depression. Some psychiatrists also have training and expertise in psychotherapy and can provide both medication management and psychotherapy.

Primary Care Physician

A primary care physician is a medical doctor, often specializing in internal medicine or family medicine. The role of your primary care physician is to monitor your medical stability, such as your vital signs, lab work, and blood levels. Ideally, you should choose a physician who is knowledgeable about eating disorders and their possible medical complications. While all four of these treatment team members are important to your recovery, maintaining routine care with your primary care physician is particularly important, because of the numerous physical complications that can occur both in the midst of your eating disorder and throughout your recovery.

You Count Too!

Each of these four members of your team is important to your recovery, but the most integral and active member of your team needs to be YOU! In order for your treatment and recovery to be successful, you need to be actively involved and informed about your eating disorder and the recovery process. It is up to you to integrate the team's recommendations into your everyday life. How can you do this? Check out some tips below.

Make Recovery a Top Priority

Recovery is time consuming! Depending on your individual situation, how often you meet with your various treatment team members will vary. It is likely that while in recovery, you might meet with your psychotherapist once or twice per week for forty-five- to sixty-minute sessions, your dietitian or nutritionist once a week (or maybe just once a month) for thirty-minute to sixty-minute sessions, your psychiatrist once a month for fifteen to thirty minutes, and your primary care physician as needed, depending on medical stability and the presence of any physical symptoms or concerns. That may seem like a lot of time, but it is important for you to make recovery an important part of your schedule. This way, you will be less likely to disregard appointments when you are busy, tired, or overwhelmed, a pattern likely to contribute to undermining the success of your recovery.

Schedule Appointments

Using the information in this chapter and in the appendix Resources (found at the back of the book), take some time to research some providers whom you can contact to create your outpatient treatment team. If you have been in an inpatient or partial hospitalization program, the professionals you worked with there can also give you referrals for outpatient providers. If possible, call several providers from each discipline. A brief phone conversation can help you get a feel for each person's personality and therapeutic style, and it gives you a chance to ask questions that will help you make an informed decision (the list of questions for psychotherapists earlier in this chapter is a good place to start). Once you have decided on your team members and have your first appointments scheduled, write down the following information.

Psychotherapist

Name: _____

Phone Number: _____

Address: _____

Appointment Date and Time: _____

Dietitian

Name: _____

Phone Number: _____

Address: _____

Appointment Date and Time: _____

Psychiatrist

Name: _____

Phone Number: _____

Address: _____

Appointment Date and Time: _____

Primary Care Physician

Name: _____

Phone Number: _____

Address: _____

Appointment Date and Time: _____

Other (e.g., Group Therapist, Art Therapist)

Name: _____

Phone Number: _____

Address: _____

Appointment Date and Time: _____

Attend All of Your Appointments

It is important that you commit yourself to your recovery and meet regularly with your team. Of course, conflicts can come up (e.g., lack of finances, scheduling conflict, illness), but it is important that you maintain an open line of communication with your team members and reschedule any missed appointments as soon as possible.

Be Honest with Your Team

Update each of them regularly about any eating disordered behaviors, feelings, or thoughts that you are experiencing. If you are not honest and up front about your situation, your team cannot help you. If you are having trouble being honest, try exploring by yourself or with your team members what is holding you back.

Listen to Your Team Members

Your eating disorder will often try to tell you to go against your team's recommendations: *Exercising just once won't hurt. They are overshooting my ideal weight range—I don't need to gain any more weight. Those coping skills won't work for me.* However, it is imperative that you follow the recommendations of your team members, as they are the experts, have experience in the common pitfalls of recovery, and have your best interest in mind.

Find Your Voice

If you are concerned about a recommendation or disagree with a suggestion, bring it up with your treatment team. Communicate your concerns and try to understand their perspective while expressing your viewpoint. Collaboration throughout your recovery enables you to actively join your team in fighting your eating disorder rather than taking a passive stance.

These are just a few ways in which you can be an active part of your recovery. What ways can *you* be active in your recovery? Each individual is different. Which of these ways (or what others) are most important for you to do to be an integral part of your team? Check out Destiny's response below before reflecting on your own ideas.

Destiny: *Being an active part of my team means that I take responsibility into my own hands a lot of the time. I have contacted a new team to support me and encourage me, but it is up to me to follow my meal plan and not use the behaviors I used before, like overexercising. It's also up to me to keep my appointments even when I want to give up.*

Now, write your ideas below:

_____

_____

_____

_____

_____

_____

Potential Pitfalls

Destiny has encountered several potential barriers in her ability to get adequate care for her eating disorder on an outpatient basis. For example, she is unable to afford a dietitian, and she is unsure if she will be able to pay for her psychotherapist. She is also ambivalent about continuing with treatment, despite her continued difficulty with relationships, communication, and depression, and she wants to try recovery on her own for a short time in order to take a break from treatment. Similarly, there are a variety of factors that may limit you in finding adequate care for your eating disorder, including financial concerns, few resources in your geographic area, ambivalence about continuing treatment, and getting stuck in self-defeating thoughts or behaviors.

Potential Pitfall 1—Limited Finances

Eating disorders are extremely expensive to treat because they require multiple providers to be involved. However, it is important to not be immediately discouraged and to take time to explore your options. If you have insurance, go online or call your insurance company to determine your physical health, mental health, and nutritional health benefits. Ask about your coverage for both in-network and out-of-network providers. In-network providers are those who accept your insurance. Typically, with an in-network provider, you will be required to pay a co-payment at the time of each of your appointments, and the health care professional will then bill the insurance company directly for the outstanding balance. Out-of-network providers do not take your insurance. However, if you have out-of-network benefits, you may still be able to get coverage; it is just slightly more complicated than with in-network providers. First, you may be required by your provider to pay the full amount for the appointment up front. Then, after someone submits an insurance claim to the insurance company (this responsibility typically falls on you as the consumer, though some health care professionals will provide this service for you), you can be reimbursed for the amount that your insurance covers. When considering including out-of-network providers on your team, it is important to first check with your insurance company to confirm how much of the fees will be covered under your insurance policy.

Even if you do not have insurance or you cannot or do not want to choose any of the providers who take your insurance, there are still some options. For example, you can ask potential treatment team members if they will work with you on a sliding scale, providing services for a reduced fee, based on your financial situation and ability to pay. You can also see if providers would be willing to see you pro bono, meaning they offer free services to those who cannot afford treatment. Below are several lists of questions that can help you explore your options for dealing with limited finances. This questionnaire is also available at http://www.newharbinger.com/39348.

Questions to Ask Regarding Outpatient Providers Who Take Your Insurance

1. What are my in-network benefits for

   a. Primary care physicians? _____

   b. Outpatient mental health professionals (specify if you are seeing a psychologist, licensed counselor, or social worker)? _____

   c. Outpatient dietitians or nutritionists? _____

2. If you have particular providers in mind, ask if they are in-network. _____

3. If you do not have particular providers in mind, ask if there is a website you can visit to find in-network providers near you. _____

4. What is my co-payment for each of these providers? _____

5. Is there a deductible I need to reach before the benefits kick in? How much has been met this year? _____

6. How many sessions will my insurance cover per year? _____

7. Is pre-authorization required? _____

   a. If so, what information do you need for this? _____

   _____

   b. Is there a specific form that needs to be filled out? _____

   c. To whom and how is this form submitted? _____

   _____

Questions to Ask Regarding Outpatient Providers Who Do Not Take Your Insurance

1. Do I have out-of-network benefits? _____

2. What are my out-of-network benefits for

    a. Primary care physicians? _____

    b. Outpatient mental health professionals (specify if you are seeing a psychologist, licensed counselor, or social worker)? _____

    c. Outpatient dietitians or nutritionists? _____

3. What percentage of the fee is reimbursed for each of these providers? _____

4. Is there a deductible I need to reach before the benefits kick in? How much has been met this year? _____

5. Is there a session limit? _____

6. Is pre-authorization required? _____

    a. If so, what information do you need for this? _____

        _____

    b. Is there a specific form that needs to be filled out? _____

    c. To whom and how is this form submitted? _____

        _____

7. What information is required to submit a claim? _____

    _____

8. Where should I send the claim information? _____

    _____

Questions to Ask Pro Bono Providers

1. Is there a limit to the number of sessions I can see you? _____

2. If I choose to see you after my allotted free sessions, will you work with me on a sliding scale? How much would I be expected to pay? _____

    _____

Potential Pitfall 2—Limited Available Resources

Another potential barrier to finding adequate treatment is a lack of resources in your area. It is possible, particularly if you live in a rural area, that the kinds of providers needed to treat eating disorders are simply not available. If you find yourself in this situation, it is important not to fall into all-or-nothing thinking. That is, rather than assuming that recovery is impossible, because you do not have access to all the treatment team members described above, keep an open mind and explore alternatives.

Although it is ideal to have a physician, a psychotherapist, a dietitian, and a psychiatrist involved in your treatment, you do not need to have all of them. If you have only a psychotherapist and a physician, take advantage of them! Some primary care physicians are very knowledgeable about medications for anxiety and depression, as well as nutritional counseling. Ask your primary care physician about his or her experience in these areas of treatment when you first meet.

Also, consider expanding your search to treatment providers who do not necessarily specialize in eating disorders. While it is generally best to find someone who has expertise and experience in working with individuals with eating disorders, it is not necessary. When contacting potential providers, be up front about being in recovery from an eating disorder and allow them to determine if they would be able to provide adequate care to you. For help in finding a treatment provider, refer to the appendix Resources at the end of this book.

Potential Pitfall 3—Ambivalence About Treatment

You may have times when you think that continuing treatment is unnecessary, that you can recover without a treatment team, that your eating disorder is not "bad enough" to warrant or deserve treatment, or that your eating disorder has been cured following intensive treatment. It is important to remember that research shows that even if you no longer meet the criteria for a formal diagnosis of anorexia, you will likely still struggle to maintain recovery and prevent relapse (Berkman et al. 2006; Cockell, Zaitsoff, and Geller 2004). Being "in recovery" is an in-between period—you're no longer acutely ill, but you've not yet recovered. Recovery is a *process* of improving yourself, of decreasing eating disordered behaviors and thoughts and improving the quality of your life. During the recovery process, you might slip up at times. Your treatment team members provide extra—and more objective—sets of eyes to help keep you from slipping to the point that you relapse. And remember that just because you may no longer meet the criteria for anorexia does not mean that your journey to a healthy and meaningful life is over; everyone can use support, especially during the difficult and vulnerable time that is recovery. Throughout your recovery journey, there are some common difficulties and struggles you might face that warrant maintaining your outpatient treatment team.

Engaging in eating disordered behaviors. Although you are in recovery and may be abstaining from using eating disordered behaviors, slips are common. You may purge, overdo it at the gym, or skip a meal "just once." However, these "just once" instances can turn into habits. It is important to accept that recovery comes with slips; be honest with your outpatient team, and work with them on improving these behaviors.

Dealing with restoring your weight to a healthy level. Getting to and maintaining a healthy weight (often referred to as being *weight restored*) can be a scary and uncomfortable experience. It will take time to accept, like, and possibly love your body at a healthy weight. Being able to express feelings of discomfort and fear with your team is important in dealing with these emotions and thoughts. Your team can help validate and challenge distorted thinking you have surrounding your weight.

Struggling to cope with life outside of intensive treatment and reintegrating back into your roles in society. If you are coming out of intensive treatment, it will take time to adjust to the reduced level of support and structure than you have been used to. Additionally, reengaging relationships and fulfilling roles that may have been on hold while you were in intensive treatment may prove to be a challenge. All of these challenges are normal and a part of the recovery process that you can address with the ongoing support of your treatment team.

Body image disturbances. Regardless of whether you are in the process of regaining weight or you are maintaining a healthy weight, body image distortions tend to linger during recovery. Your body may have regained its health, but your mind takes longer to recover. It is common to struggle with perceiving your body and yourself as heavy, ugly, or worthless. It is important to address these body image disturbances with the help of your team, particularly with your psychotherapist.

Struggling with your mood and anxieties. While your eating patterns and behaviors may have improved, your underlying mood disturbances and anxieties may take longer to resolve. Eating disorders tend to numb intense emotions and therefore are a way of coping with such emotions. When those coping mechanisms are taken away, you will likely feel intense levels of mood instability, depression, or anxiety until you learn to identify your emotions and develop new skills to respond to and manage your feelings. Your treatment team is important in aiding you to healthily accept, express, and deal with your emotions.

Building and maintaining a social network. Eating disorders often cause you to isolate yourself from friends and family, but having an active support system and social network is important for your recovery. Forming these relationships will likely be a scary—and perhaps new—experience for you. Many times, what inhibits you from forming relationships has to do with how you think and feel about yourself. Your treatment team can help you understand the underlying reasons these situations are scary for you, how to try new ways of meeting people, and how to rebuild relationships that diminished while you were actively engaging in your eating disorder.

Dealing with past traumas. If you experienced a trauma in the past, such as abuse, sexual assault, or neglect, it is likely still affecting how you feel, think, and interact with others. Because eating disorders often serve as a means of coping, the symptoms of trauma (e.g., nightmares, flashbacks, heightened anxiety) could resurface when your eating disorder is no longer numbing your emotions. It is important to deal with these types of issues in continued psychotherapy to prevent them from triggering a relapse.

Learning to communicate your needs in a healthy way. When you were active in your eating disorder, you likely used your body as a means of coping with and expressing your emotions and needs. You may have starved yourself as a way of saying, "Help! Something is wrong." In order to steer clear of this problem, you need to work with your psychotherapist to develop and practice new ways of communicating with others and meeting your emotional, physical, and social needs.

Potential Pitfall 4—Self-Defeating Cycles

Recovery can be difficult, requiring a lot of effort, time, and attention. It is likely that you will go through times when you want to take a break from recovery—or give up entirely. It is during times like these that you are more likely to do and think things that will hinder your progress. These are often called *self-defeating cycles* because they keep you stuck rather than moving forward in your recovery. There are many examples of self-defeating cycles that you may find yourself in:

- You may keep secrets, or you may lie to your team about your behaviors. You may avoid talking about how much you are eating. You may lie about how much time you are spending exercising or how often you are purging. You may find yourself minimizing problematic behaviors to yourself, thinking things like *I can handle it, I just did that once, I can control this,* or *I'm doing better than others I know, so this isn't so bad.*

- It is also common for you to disagree, sometimes strongly, with your team members about your ideal weight or how your body is perceived by others. Despite what they say, you may insist that you are too heavy or fat. You may focus too much on convincing your treatment team that you are too big, perhaps as a way of avoiding dealing with deeper issues. Or you minimize your team's concern about your weight simply to avoid facing the reality that you may need to gain weight.

- For one reason or another, you may lose trust in your team members and perceive them as not taking your needs seriously. At times like these, you may believe that you understand your needs better than your team members.

- You might begin to believe that you are different from everyone else, so you do not need to follow treatment recommendations that "apply only to others." You may think, *What works for others will not work for me, so why try?* or *I've already tried these skills. They didn't work then; why would they work now?*

- Because of these difficulties, you may not follow your team's advice regarding your treatment. You may disregard suggestions about the appropriate level of care, become defensive toward challenges to your distorted thinking, and develop a "nothing is ever going to work" attitude.

It takes a lot of self-awareness to recognize when you are falling into cognitive and behavioral patterns like these. Not only is it important to maintain contact with your treatment team and discuss your problems with them in order to understand why you are feeling hopeless and want to give up, it is also important to engage in self-reflection. For example, ask yourself, *What underlying feelings am I experiencing that are driving my frustrations with my team and recovery? Besides my dissatisfaction with my weight and eating, what else could be contributing to this shift in my attitude?* and *What am I gaining from taking a break from recovery?* Reflect on these types of questions both alone and in session with your psychotherapist. Take a step back before making rash decisions about your treatment, and try to make decisions that will be best for you and your recovery.

Finally, determining how often you need to meet with your team members may be an area of concern as you go through the recovery process. The frequency with which you meet with them—and the particular decision to meet less frequently as you make progress—is a collaborative decision that should only be made after engaging in honest self-reflection and open and frank discussion with them. You and your team members should work together to determine when you are ready to meet less frequently. Important factors to take into consideration include psychological stability, physical stability (weight and vitals), medical stability (no recent or unforeseen changes in your medications), motivation, self-reliance (the consistency with which you're following your meal plan), frequency of behaviors, accountability of behaviors, finances, and insurance coverage.

Overall, it has been shown that individuals benefit from continued psychotherapy through the recovery process (Berkman et al. 2006). Maintaining recovery is often a difficult feat, and relapse is common, putting your physical, emotional, psychological, and interpersonal well-being at risk. Thus, continuing and engaging in treatment to maintain recovery and prevent relapse is of great importance, and it is a great investment in yourself and your future. Ideally, engagement in treatment will continue until both you and your treatment team determine that you no longer need the support of a team.

Journaling Pages

In this chapter, we discussed the importance of creating and maintaining an outpatient team and explored who the most crucial treatment team members are. We also highlighted common pitfalls and barriers to adequate treatment. What pitfalls do you feel may be most difficult for you to overcome? Which ones have you experienced in the past? Use the space below to reflect on your recovery, identifying which pitfalls or barriers are most likely to be present in your journey. As you list each one, brainstorm some potential solutions and highlight the struggles you are having difficulty overcoming. Perhaps you can talk with a treatment provider, family member, or friend about your concerns.

_____

_____

_____

_____

_____

_____

_____

_____

_____

_____

_____

_____

_____

_____

Chapter 3

Transitions After Intensive Treatment

One can choose to go back toward safety or forward toward growth. Growth must be chosen again and again; fear must be overcome again and again.

—Abraham Maslow

Meet Brad

Brad was discharged from a residential eating disorders program two weeks ago. He spent three months in residential treatment and worked really hard to make progress. When he was admitted to the hospital, he was binge eating, purging, and restricting his eating. He despised his body and was isolated from friends. While in residential treatment, he learned to balance his eating and developed coping skills that help him not purge. He has now stepped down to an outpatient team, consisting of a psychiatrist, dietitian, and psychotherapist. While he has maintained his weight and abstained from eating disordered behaviors since his discharge, he has been struggling with strong urges to purge after meals. He feels significant pressure from his parents to integrate quickly back into school next month, but he feels like he is already having difficulty balancing the everyday demands in his life (his physical and mental health appointments, reintegrating back into his social circle and explaining his absence, following his meal plan, and fighting urges to engage in eating disordered behaviors). He is still learning how to openly and effectively communicate with his family, so he has not been able to explain his fears about not being able to return to a "normal" life. Brad is trying to be patient with himself and not give up, because he desperately wants to maintain the progress he has made over the past three months. However, he worries and at times feels hopeless about his ability to continue being successful in recovery.

Challenges During Transition

For many people, transitioning from intensive treatment (such as a residential facility or partial hospitalization program) back into the "real world" can be quite challenging. The decrease in support and structure can make it difficult to maintain and continue the progress you made in intensive treatment. After having support for twelve or twenty-four hours per day, you're now seeing your treatment team just a few hours each week. It takes some time to get used to this shift, and like Brad, you will likely encounter some challenges during this transition period, which can last several months. Over the next several pages, we will explore some areas where you may encounter difficulty as you transition in treatment. In each area, we will discuss the type of challenge you may face, pose some questions for consideration, and allow you space to write your thoughts.

Eating Behavior

Although Brad has maintained his weight by following his meal plan, he spends a lot of time planning and preparing meals, and he worries about being able to keep up this effort in the future. Following and completing your meal plan on your own can be extremely difficult. The responsibility is all yours. Before, you were motivated to follow your plan partly because clinicians were watching you and holding you accountable, and you didn't want to lose privileges in the treatment center. But now your motivation has to be internal; you must follow your plan because you value your health and recovery. What challenges do you foresee or have you experienced regarding your eating habits? What motivates you to follow your meal plan?

_____

_____

_____

_____

Managing Urges and Behaviors

Brad's strong urges to purge have increased since his discharge. Despite not engaging in these behaviors, the urges leave him feeling discouraged about his success in recovery. With less structure and supervision, you may also struggle to refrain from engaging in eating disordered behaviors like restricting, bingeing, and purging, as well as other behaviors, such as exercising, counting calories, or engaging in food rituals. What urges and eating disordered behaviors have been most challenging for you to manage? What tends to impact your urges or engagement in these types of behaviors the most?

_____

_____

_____

_____

Maintaining Weight

If you struggle to follow your meal plan or you engage in eating disordered behaviors after you leave intensive treatment, you may have difficulty maintaining a healthy weight. Similarly, the temptation of weighing yourself excessively (or at all, depending on your team's recommendations) may be great, as you likely have more access to a scale. What struggles have you faced regarding your relationship with your weight?

_____

_____

_____

_____

Balancing Demands

Brad is worried about being able to balance all the demands of his life, like school and socializing, while still focusing on recovery. It is likely that as you come out of intensive treatment, you are also hoping to or expected to go back to work or school. It may take some time to get used to this shift in daily activity and routine. It is common for this shift to feel overwhelming and for you to struggle to keep your recovery a priority in the midst of reintegrating back into work and schooling. What challenges in balancing various aspects of your life and recovery do you anticipate or have you already encountered? In your list of priorities, where does recovery rank?

_____

_____

_____

_____

Self-Care

In transitioning out of intensive treatment, it may be difficult for you to make time for yourself. In intensive treatment, you were likely encouraged daily to take time to engage in self-care activities to improve your mood and well-being. However, it is now up to you to create a balance in your life that includes both fulfilling your responsibilities and taking time to take care of yourself and have fun. How do you feel you are balancing responsibilities and self-care? What ways are you taking time to engage in self-care? What are some barriers to taking care of yourself?

_____

_____

_____

_____

Building Relationships

For Brad, rebuilding relationships is a priority, but he has struggled in this area. Prior to treatment, he was isolated and refused to go out to meals with his friends. Now he worries what he will talk about with them when they go out. Similarly, you may experience difficulty socializing once you transition out of intensive treatment. It is common to feel disconnected from others in your life. Isolation is common in individuals with anorexia, and that can be made more severe during and after intensive treatment. You may have put many relationships on hold, and rebuilding them takes time and effort. You may also have difficulty finding time to socialize while you are focusing on recovery and integrating back into your various life roles (student, family member, friend, employee). What challenges have come up for you in this area? What difficult feelings or thoughts do you experience in social situations? Why is it important to you to reestablish relationships in your life? How might these relationships be helpful to you in your recovery?

_____

_____

_____

_____

Shame and Embarrassment

Not all of Brad's friends know he was in treatment for the past three months, and he worries about how to explain where he has been. He is uncomfortable talking with people about his eating disorder and does not know how to respond when people ask why he was away for so long. It is also possible that you will struggle with shame or embarrassment. There are a variety of circumstances that can elicit these feelings, such as needing to explain your absence from work or school, the discomfort of having gained weight, and not being "cured" as you continue to have struggles outside of intensive treatment. What are some of your sources of shame or embarrassment? In what situations are these feelings most present for you?

Motivation

During the months following intensive treatment, there will likely be times when you feel yourself losing motivation. There will be difficult days and weeks, and you may sometimes feel like giving up, while at other times you will feel highly motivated. Check in with yourself in this moment; on a scale of 0 to 100 (with 100 being the most), how motivated are you feeling in your recovery? _____. What is currently having a negative impact on your level of motivation? Since motivation varies over time, what are some factors that impact your motivation (both positively and negatively)?

Expectations

Brad's parents are excited about his recovery, and they believe getting back to "life" quickly is best for him. However, Brad worries that he is not ready to take on all the responsibilities and hardships that contributed to his eating disorder in the first place. Moving back home after intensive treatment is likely to be a big adjustment. You may need to acclimate to having others' schedules to consider, feeling pressure from family or friends to consistently eat or exercise "normally," or having to explain why certain things others do or say (e.g., having a scale in the house, skipping breakfast) are triggering for you. What expectations do others have for you now that you have returned from intensive treatment? What adjustments are most difficult for you in returning home?

_____

_____

_____

_____

Triggers

While dealing with triggers will likely be an ongoing process for a long time, in the months immediately following intensive treatment it can be particularly difficult. In intensive treatment, exposure to triggers is controlled to some degree; in the real world, they may be all around you. Your friends may go to the gym, while you are not supposed to be exercising. A family member might be dieting. You may hear people engaging in fat talk. Everyone finds different experiences triggering, and they can be difficult to manage without resorting to eating disordered behaviors to cope. What kinds of everyday triggers do you find most difficult to be around? How are you currently managing these triggers? How would you like to manage them?

_____

_____

_____

_____

Recognizing and Being Proud of Your Progress

Despite the difficulties you face as you transition out of intensive treatment, it can be helpful to recognize and appreciate the progress you have made thus far. Taking time to acknowledge your positive steps and accomplishments throughout recovery can help you gain a sense of self-efficacy. Performing tasks successfully helps you feel more confident and capable of achieving your goals and helps you maintain motivation (*If I was able to not overexercise for three months, I can do it for another three months. I have conquered my fear of eating ten fear foods; I'm going to try to get to fifteen. I'm no longer freezing and dizzy all the time. And regardless of how strong my urges to act on eating disordered behaviors are, I will not act on them because I do not want to go back to feeling like that.*). It is common to focus solely on your daily struggles and what is going wrong in recovery; but that can leave you feeling stuck. Taking time to remind yourself of your progress is helpful for both your attitude toward and your motivation for recovery. Below are some questions about the progress you've made during recovery so far. Read Brad's answers, and then reflect and write down your thoughts on the questions.

1.   What physical complications or symptoms have resolved or improved?

Brad: *Before treatment I was always cold, my nails were brittle, and my hair would fall out. I felt bloated, I struggled with acid reflux, and sitting for long periods of time was painful. Although this has improved a lot since beginning treatment, I still experience constipation and reflux sometimes.*

You: _____

_____

_____

2.   In what ways has your mood improved? What steps have you taken to help improve your mood?

Brad: *I started a new medication for my anxiety and depression, which has helped a lot. My psychotherapist and I also worked together and found some coping skills (like coloring and drawing, journaling, squeezing a stress ball, deep breathing) that are really helpful when my emotions get really intense. I used to become incredibly moody and irritable when I was starving, so eating regularly has helped improve my mood. Even though I still struggle with anxiety, my depression is much better, I feel more energetic, I don't cry as often, and I don't think about suicide anymore.*

You: _____

_____

_____

3.   What coping skills have you developed?

Brad: *I learned that creating art is extremely therapeutic for me. I also learned to communicate better and to voice my needs. I enjoy journaling, writing poetry, and going out for coffee with my friends as well.*

You: _____

_____

_____

4.   How has your relationship with food improved?

Brad: *I still don't feel completely comfortable around food, but my relationship with it has definitely improved! I don't have an all-or-nothing relationship with food anymore. Before treatment, I would either not eat anything or binge, but now I feel like I really learned how to follow a meal plan, which helps me maintain a balance. I have maintained my weight on my current meal plan for almost a month now, so I'm beginning to believe that consuming calories is not going to make me fat.*

You: _____

_____

_____

5.   What fear foods (foods you have avoided out of some anxiety or fear) have you successfully eaten?

Brad: *I have been able to eat almost all the junk food, like chips and cookies, that I previously feared without bingeing. I also have successfully integrated caloric drinks into my meals.*

You: _____

_____

_____

6. In what ways has your body image improved? What steps have you taken to improve your body image?

Brad: *While I'm not yet at the point where I love my body, I have gone from despising my body to tolerating it. I think what has helped the most has been defining what I value outside my eating disorder, such as friendships and nature, and engaging in those things. With the help of my psychotherapist, I also learned to practice acceptance of my poor body-image thoughts. This has been and will continue to be helpful, because I try to just notice them rather than let them upset me.*

You: _____

_____

_____

7. How have you improved in terms of acting on eating disordered behaviors?

Brad: *I haven't purged or restricted my food intake for two months now. I still have urges, but I have done really well with not acting on them!*

You: _____

_____

_____

8. How have your connections with others improved? What steps have you taken to improve your relationships with others?

Brad: *I was pretty isolated from my friends before entering treatment. Once I felt better, I made efforts to reconnect with my friends by calling them and video chatting with them during my free time. I still struggle with anxiety about being left out, but my relationships with my friends have improved a lot. As for my relationship with my parents, I still feel tense around them, but we are working on communicating better, which has helped us feel more connected as a family.*

You: _____

_____

_____

9.   How has your relationship with yourself improved? What steps have you taken to improve how you feel about yourself?

Brad: *I'm learning to be compassionate and patient with myself, which is completely new to me. For as long as I can remember, I have disliked myself and always focused on my flaws. I'm making efforts to appreciate my positive qualities and to do things that help me feel competent and likeable, such as creating art, calling friends, and initiating plans. This is extremely hard and uncomfortable for me, but I keep pushing myself to do this. I'm trying to trust my team members, who keep telling me that it will get easier and more natural with time.*

You: _____

_____

_____

Completing this exercise requires time, mental effort, and insight. It is possible that you are struggling to come up with answers to some of these questions. After answering the questions yourself, it may also be useful to ask close friends, family, or treatment team members about the questions and your answers. Perhaps they see changes in you that you are not yet aware of, and their perspective may help you become more aware of your progress. Regardless of how long you spent in intensive treatment, you have likely made some amount of progress, and you should be proud of it! As you continue through recovery, reflect back on these questions again and take the time to appreciate your continued progress.

There Is Still Progress to Be Made

While it is important to recognize and appreciate how far you have come in recovery, it is also vital to be aware of the progress you still have to make. Perhaps you have an idea of the steps that you still need to take, or maybe you feel completely lost now that you are out of intensive treatment. On the following pages is a list to help guide you in recognizing aspects of recovery that you can continue to improve upon. The list is quite comprehensive, addressing recovery both from eating disordered behaviors and thoughts and from general mental health difficulties that may impact or coexist with your eating disorder. Before you continue, remember that everyone's recovery is different and that there is no such thing as a perfect recovery. Not every indicator of recovery listed below may be applicable or relevant to you. Likewise, this is not a comprehensive list, and there may be other steps that you need to take in recovery.

Highlight or underline the recovery indicators on the list that pertain to you. This will help you organize your thoughts for an activity presented later in the chapter. It is also important to remember that most of these indicators are not all or nothing. Many of them exist on a continuum. For example, you do not simply "have" or "not have" positive self-esteem; self-esteem can range from "very low" to "very high," and it can vary over time. Similarly, while having no fear foods is ideal, depending on where you are in your recovery, a decrease in the number of foods that you are scared of eating or a decrease in your level of fear around certain foods may be indicative of positive steps in recovery. Keeping that in mind, as you go through this list, ask yourself, *How do I need to improve (or continue improving) in this area for my recovery to be successful?* Don't think of each indicator as an item on a checklist that is simply achieved or not. Many of these concepts are explained and discussed in detail later on in this workbook. If you are confused by or unsure how any of the ideas presented in this list may apply to you, consult with your psychotherapist.

Physical Health

- You are working on gaining weight, or you have achieved and are maintaining a healthy weight.

- Your labs and vital signs are stabilizing and returning to normal.

- Your engagement in restricting, purging, overexercising, and using laxatives or diuretics has been significantly reduced or stopped.

Nutritional Well-Being

- You are working on following the meal plan your dietitian has set for you.

- You are more able to recognize when you are hungry and full.

- You are increasingly able to eat a variety of foods and do not restrict the types of foods you eat.

- You have significantly reduced the number of foods that you avoid or are scared of eating.

- You are better able to eat in social situations, such as at restaurants, with friends or family, and at parties.

Emotional and Mental Health

- Your view of yourself and your self-esteem has improved.

- You are working on accepting and loving your body. You are also better able to view yourself more accurately without a grossly distorted body image.

- Your acceptance of the weight you should be for your body to be healthy and fully functioning is increasing.

- You have significantly decreased the amount of time you spend thinking about food (e.g., you are able to eat without ruminating about it afterward).

- You experience significantly less anxiety or discomfort when cooking, preparing, eating, or being around food.

- You have more flexibility in your daily routine and are better able to adapt to changes to your schedule.

- Your mood has become more stable, and you are increasingly able to identify and express your emotions in a healthy and timely manner. You are also better able to validate your own feelings and allow yourself to feel a full range of emotions.

- You are better at recognizing when you need help and are able ask for it.

- You are more able to recognize when you are slipping and are honest about it with others.

- You take more responsibility for your actions, particularly with regard to engaging in eating disordered behaviors.

- You are developing and implementing healthy coping skills and use them regularly in response to difficult emotions, thoughts, and situations.

- You have a low to moderate level of perfectionism. You are better able to accept occasional failure and are satisfied with being "normal" rather than "the best."

- You are more comfortable respecting and expressing your sexuality as it pertains to your age and values.

- You have an improving sense of who you are, and you are more able to identify yourself in a variety of healthy domains (e.g., a student, a sister, someone who loves to paint). Your self-worth comes more from who you are as a person rather than your weight and body shape and size.

- You are better able to recognize when you are comparing yourself to others, particularly with regard to appearance. You are more accepting of yourself and understand and believe your core worth is not based on how you compare to others.

- You regularly take time for yourself and engage in self-care activities that make your life balanced, meaningful, and whole.

- You feel less guilt, shame, or embarrassment regarding your body, your eating habits, or yourself as a whole.

Social and Interpersonal Well-Being

- You are working on finding a middle ground between being passive and being aggressive, and you are better able to advocate for yourself.

- Your ability to resolve conflict in a healthy and appropriate manner is improving. You rely less on using your body to express yourself or control or manipulate the situation during conflicts with others.

- You engage in social situations more often and have more fulfilling and meaningful social relationships.

- You are better able to recognize the limitations of your family members and your relationships with them, and you are learning healthy ways of interacting with them.

- You can better identify and set healthy boundaries with others in your life.

- You are more able to engage in and feel comfortable in intimate relationships.

- You are working on striking a healthy balance between depending on others and asserting your independence.

- Your support network has improved in quality or quantity (or both), depending on your needs.

Now, take some time to reflect on where you are in your recovery regarding these indicators by completing the Well-Being Wheel that follows. In the inner circle, list ways in which you have improved within each domain. Be specific and try to address as many of the indicators you highlighted or underlined as possible; also add any indicators that were not on the list but you recognize as being important in your case. Then, in the outer circle, list ways in which you want or need to continue to improve. Again, be as specific as possible. Brad completed a sample for you to use as guidance. This exercise is also available at http://www.newharbinger.com/39348.

Brad's Well-Being Wheel

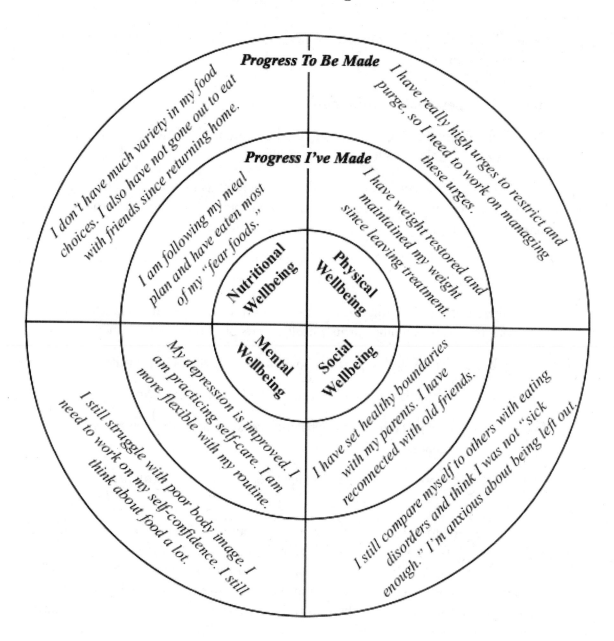

Progress To Be Made

I have really high urges to restrict and purge, so I need to work on managing these urges.

I don't have much variety in my food choices. I also have not gone out to eat with friends since returning home.

Progress I've Made

I have weight restored and maintained my weight since leaving treatment.

I am following my meal plan and have eaten most of my "fear foods."

Nutritional Wellbeing

Physical Wellbeing

Mental Wellbeing

Social Wellbeing

My depression is improved. I am practicing self-care. I am more flexible with my routine.

I have set healthy boundaries with my parents. I have reconnected with old friends.

I still struggle with poor body image. I need to work on my self-confidence. I still think about food a lot.

I still compare myself to others with eating disorders and think I was not "sick enough." I'm anxious about being left out.

Your Well-Being Wheel

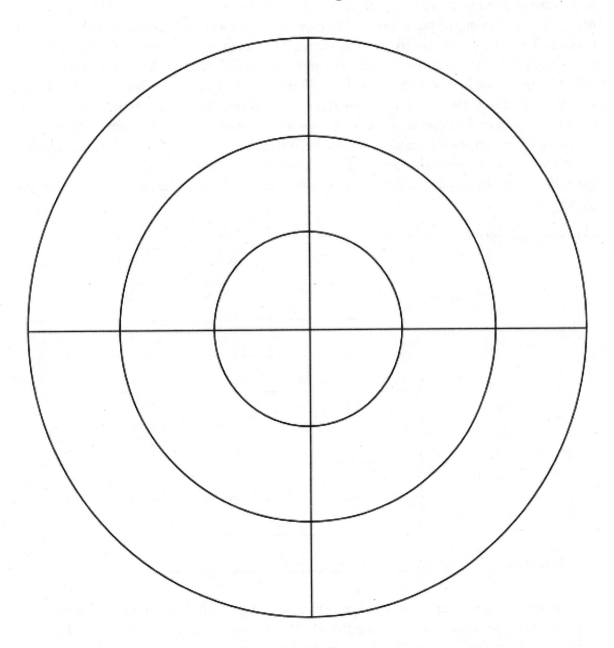

Striking a balance between progress made and progress that needs to be made is important, as focusing only on your successes may leave you in denial and keep you from fully recovering, while focusing only on the areas you need to improve on can leave you feeling overwhelmed and hopeless. You may also want to try creating a list of priorities for each indicator of recovery, so you can clarify what elements are most (and least) important to address. You and your treatment team will often be working toward several goals simultaneously, so this may be helpful in prioritizing your goals. However, if you are going to use this list therapeutically, it is important to consult your team members regarding how your priorities align with what they feel is most important for you.

Using the information from your Well-Being Wheel, list below what you believe needs to be addressed in order for you to be successful in recovery. You may choose to do this in session with the help of your psychotherapist or on your own to discuss with your treatment team members at a later time.

Most Important   1. _____

                        2. _____

                        3. _____

                        4. _____

                        5. _____

                        6. _____

                        7. _____

                        8. _____

                        9. _____

Least Important   10. _____

It is possible that your ideas on what is most important will differ from your team's. For example, you may think that improving the stability of your mood is most important, but your team may suggest that getting to a healthy weight is most important, as your physical health may be negatively impacting your mental health and therefore needs to be of greater focus. Ideally, you and your treatment team can negotiate and agree on a particular hierarchy. There may continue to be occasional disagreements, and it is important to take those opportunities to voice your concerns, practice finding a balance between advocating for yourself and trusting your team's judgment, and following their recommendations.

Journaling Pages

In this chapter, we discussed common challenges faced in the months following intensive treatment, as well as common indicators of recovery. You also explored the progress you have made in your recovery and the progress you still need to make. As Abraham Maslow's quote at the beginning of this chapter makes clear, growth and overcoming fear need to be chosen over and over again throughout a journey. How is this relevant to you and to your recovery process? What is this journey like for you? What are some of your goals for this journey, and how are you hoping to see it move forward toward growth? In what ways are you working toward overcoming fear? Below, please write any other thoughts, feelings, ideas, concerns, and issues that you are thinking about or experiencing. These can be reflected on over time and discussed with your psychotherapist.

Chapter 4

Understanding Your Eating Disorder

Understanding is the first step to acceptance, and only with acceptance can there be recovery.

—J. K. Rowling

Meet Kate

Kate has been working on her recovery for several years now. Throughout her treatment, she has made significant progress in making sense of her eating disorder, understanding what contributed to it, and gaining insight into what prevents her from maintaining recovery. With her psychotherapist, she has pieced together a coherent set of factors that have influenced her eating disorder. She recently summarized her insights in a brief essay, which she shared in a support group she attends. Her essay reads:

It has been a long road up until this point, and I think I have finally gained an understanding of my eating disorder. Growing up, I was always more anxious than my siblings. I think I'm just hardwired to be more sensitive. I also witnessed a lot of negative body talk from my sister and mother as a kid; they seemed to constantly be talking about how fat they were or problem areas on their bodies. Because I'm more sensitive, I think I internalized these statements at a young age. I remember being hyperaware of my clothing sizes beginning in third grade, and this focus on size only increased as my friends and I hit puberty and discussion of weight was common. Around this time, my mom also got married to a man without giving my siblings and me much warning or say in the decision. I didn't really think that I made much of that at the time, but I realize now that I harbored a lot of anger about it, which I ultimately took out on myself. I felt out of control and devalued, and in a way, I think my eating disorder served as a way of forcing my mom to make me a priority. I started restricting and losing weight in high school, and after fainting in class and a visit to my doctor, who diagnosed me with anorexia, my family finally recognized the pain I was communicating through my body.

Recovery has been really hard, despite this insight. My mom is unwilling to participate in family therapy, which is hard for me, since much of my anger and communication issues are prominent in our relationship. I'm still a pretty anxious person, though it is better controlled with medication now. I also have a lot of work I need to continue on my perception of my body, as my dissatisfaction with my body is highly related to disliking myself. I've learned that I can't change my past, and I realize that I need to stop fighting with the reality of my past. I also can't change the fact that my mom won't participate in my treatment. I'm quite angry with my mom for all of this, but rather than trying to stop my anger, I'm working on acknowledging and accepting these feelings. Understanding all of this has helped me make sense of my experiences, and practicing acceptance has allowed me the space to move forward in my recovery.

Precipitating and Maintaining Factors

Why did I develop an eating disorder? Why is recovery so hard for me? These might be some of the questions that have crossed your mind since being diagnosed with anorexia. Or they may be questions that you will encounter as you progress through recovery. Either way, understanding the roots of your eating disorder can help you make sense of your experiences.

Unfortunately, there is no one thing that has been found to cause anorexia. There are many factors that contribute to the development and maintenance of eating disorders. Before reading ahead, it is important to remember that we cannot always know which factors contributed to the development of an eating disorder in the first place (these causes or triggers are called *precipitating factors*) and which conditions or stressors perpetuate and maintain your eating disorder (these are called *maintaining factors*).

Not all of the precipitating and maintaining factors in the list below apply to everyone, and this is not a comprehensive list of all factors that could be influencing your eating disorder. The purpose of this chapter is not for you to definitively know what led to you developing an eating disorder or to know for sure what is keeping you from full recovery. Instead, the information and exercises in this chapter are aimed at helping you begin to make sense of your experience with an eating disorder.

Biological Influences

- Hormones, neurotransmitters (e.g., serotonin), and stress can all affect appetite and eating habits in ways that contribute to the development of an eating disorder.

- Bodies change and react to starvation in ways that can make recovery difficult. For example, bloating and gastric discomfort can make eating uncomfortable. Starvation can also change how you smell and taste food, which can impact your appetite and eating habits.

Genetic Influences

- Genetics can be a significant risk factor for developing an eating disorder.

- Researchers estimate that about 56 to 74 percent of one's risk for developing anorexia is genetic (Bulik et al. 2006; Bulik et al. 2010; Klump et al. 2009; Wade et al. 2009).

- Relatives of a woman with anorexia nervosa are 11.3 times more likely to have anorexia than those who do not have a relative with anorexia (Strober et al. 2000).

Social and Cultural Influences

- Westernized cultures often idealize thinness, dieting, and losing weight, both in everyday interactions and through the media. Media and cultural influences do not cause eating disorders, but these factors can impact those who are genetically or psychologically vulnerable to developing an eating disorder.

- Research has found that 47 percent of American children between fifth grade and twelfth grade report wanting to lose weight because of images they see in the media, and 69 percent of this population also report that magazine images influence how they perceive the perfect body (Martin 2010).

- Peers can also influence eating behaviors, weight and body shape attitudes, and self-esteem. Whether through peer pressure, leading by example, encouragement, or teasing for not adhering to social norms, peers can have a powerful impact. For example, adolescents, particularly girls, often learn about the importance of thinness and behaviors, such as dieting, purging, and exercising, from their peers.

- Abuse, trauma, and bullying, particularly about one's body, are often linked to anorexia and are considered risk factors in developing an eating disorder.

- Stressful life events can also act as a catalyst for engaging in eating disordered behaviors. Focusing one's attention on weight and eating can be a coping mechanism, giving one a sense of emotional control.

Family Influences

- Family environments that are highly critical and have poor communication are common among those who develop eating disorders.

- Families may hyper focus on body weight and shape. Family members may also communicate spoken or unspoken messages about what is good or bad in terms of weight. For example, family members may make negative comments about their own or others' bodies.

- Family members also influence eating patterns by modeling healthy or unhealthy eating habits.

- Family comments, punishments, or reinforcements regarding appearance or eating patterns can impact one's relationship with food.

Psychological Influences

- Stress, mood disorders, and an increased level of emotional distress are often related to eating disorders. Sometimes mood issues contribute to the development of anorexia. Other times, anorexia leads to mood disturbances, as some eating disorder symptoms, such as caloric restriction, can lead to depression.

- High levels of anxiety are also common for people with anorexia. Like depression, anxiety can contribute to or result from eating disordered behaviors. For example, many people with anorexia experience a fear of humiliation and embarrassment when eating in front of others and become anxious when food is present.

- Related to anxiety, isolating oneself from social situations, particularly when food is involved, can increase more general social isolation and reinforce insecurity.

- Low self-esteem is strongly related to developing anorexia. Girls with low self-esteem are more likely to develop disordered eating patterns, and low self-esteem makes recovery particularly challenging.

- People with anorexia also tend to have issues with control. Those with anorexia often experience feelings of loss of control and gain a sense of control through their eating disordered behaviors.

- Body image issues are prominent in anorexia. People with eating disorders often do not have a realistic sense of their physical self, usually perceiving themselves as being larger than is objectively true.

- Body dissatisfaction also contributes to the development of eating disorders. Being satisfied with one's body has been shown to serve as a protective factor in adolescent girls who are otherwise at risk for developing an eating disorder (Polivy and Herman 2002).

- Your thinking style may contribute to the development and maintenance of an eating disorder.

  - You may spend a significant amount of time obsessing about food and weight.

  - You may frequently engage in rigid, all-or-nothing thinking patterns, resulting in viewing yourself negatively, as any evidence suggesting you are not perfect likely causes you to regard yourself as a failure.

  - You may be a perfectionist and interpret your minor or normal imperfections as major problems or signs of failure.

  - You may lack internal awareness, such that you are unable to accurately identify internal feelings, such as hunger or satiety. This may lead you to mistrust your body, increasing the need to control it, which can result in eating disorder symptoms.

Other Influences

- Eating disorders also tend to serve a purpose or are used as a coping mechanism.

- Your eating disorder may provide you with a sense of structure and predictability, and thus comfort. It can also be a way to feel in control, especially when other aspects of life feel out of control or chaotic.

- Your eating disorder may be a means of avoiding negative emotions and experiences and distracting yourself from life stresses. Kate, for example, found her eating disorder functioning as a way to avoid and manage her anger toward her mother and as a way to distract herself from the stress of her mother's remarriage.

- Your eating disorder may give you a sense of self-confidence, superiority, and achievement. You may associate losing weight with intelligence, attractiveness, and successfulness. Thus, by losing weight, you may feel better about yourself overall.

- As you lose weight, you may experience an inner drive, such as a rush or sense of power, which may lead to feeling that you have achieved a sense of mastery, mental strength, and self-control.

- Your eating disorder can be a way to stand out or feel important. Your eating disorder may feel like it is your only source of identity, especially if you have struggled for a long time. Because eating disorders are so consuming, it can be hard to see yourself outside your diagnosis and struggles.

- Your eating disorder may be a means of eliciting care, love, and attention from others. As you lost significant amounts of weight, those around you may have expressed concern or admiration. This expression of care and attention from family and friends is often a positive experience. You may view others' worries about you having lost weight as a demonstration of caring and love. Kate, for example, finally became a priority to her mother after becoming sick from her eating disorder.

- You may use your eating disorder as a means of communicating your difficulties to others. You may have problems expressing yourself to friends and family, and using eating disordered behaviors is a means of doing so.

After reading through this overview of potential influences on anorexia, which factors stick out for you? Which factors relate to your experience with your eating disorder? Which factors can you identify as precipitating factors? Which are your maintaining factors? Remember that some factors can be *both* precipitating and maintaining factors. Just as Kate has done below, write your ideas about what has contributed to your eating disorder. You may wish also to consult with your psychotherapist or other members of your team to help you create a comprehensive list.

Kate's Precipitating Factors

1. *Anxious temperament*

2. *Negative body talk within my family*

3. *Peers focusing on weight*

4. *Anger about my mom's marriage to my stepfather*

5. *Lack of sense of control in my life*

6. *Feeling devalued and needing attention from my mom*

7. *Needing to communicate my pain but not being able to through words*

Kate's Maintaining Factors

1. *Anxious temperament*

2. *Poor body image*

3. *My mom won't participate in family therapy to help resolve conflict*

4. *Continuing to feel unimportant because my mom won't come to therapy*

5. *Anger toward my mom*

6. *Difficulty communicating my feelings and needs to others*

7. *Poor sense of identity outside of my eating disorder*

Your Precipitating Factors

1. _____

2. _____

3. _____

4. _____

5. _____

6. _____

7. _____

Your Maintaining Factors

1. _____

2. _____

3. _____

4. _____

5. _____

6. _____

7. _____

Using Dialectical Behavior Therapy

Identifying what has likely caused your eating disorder and what is currently maintaining it is an important first step. Insight such as this can help you understand yourself; it can give you an explanation of what you have gone through and continue to go through. This insight can also help you feel less at fault, as many of these factors are likely out of your control. It also gives you a sense of what is within your control, so you can identify with your psychotherapist ways to change the things that are maintaining your eating disorder.

So what do you do with this knowledge and awareness? Before addressing that question, let's take a brief look at one of the commonly used types of psychotherapy shown to be effective in treating eating disorders, dialectical behavior therapy, or DBT (Bankoff et al. 2012). In DBT, you learn skills related to mindfulness, distress tolerance, emotion regulation, and interpersonal effectiveness (Linehan 1993). The basis of these skills stems from learning and balancing dialectics. A *dialectic* is a way of thinking about two truths that may seem like opposites. For example, *I know that I am underweight, and I also know that my brain tells me I'm chubby.* By learning to acknowledge and hold in mind two opposing truths, you are better able to accept reality as it is and move forward to make necessary changes that will help your recovery.

As part of DBT, you are encouraged to practice acceptance and change simultaneously, as each of these practices influences and helps you work on the other. Thus, it is important to *both* accept yourself in the moment *and* make changes. These practices may seem contradictory, but without one you cannot have the other. For example, if you do not value or care about yourself, you are not likely to nourish yourself in a healthy way. However, once you accept where you are in recovery and accept yourself as you currently are, you are more likely to find peace with yourself and take the steps you need to change the way you nourish yourself. This will subsequently reinforce your acceptance of yourself as you practice making the changes you need to live a healthy and meaningful life. Kate described a similar experience with acceptance when she stated: "Understanding all of this has helped me make sense of my experiences, and practicing acceptance has allowed me the space to move forward in my recovery."

Now, let's apply these concepts to the task at hand: working with your identified precipitating and maintaining factors. A common phrase in DBT is, "While I may not have caused all of my pain and problems, I am the only one who is capable of and responsible for changing them." Here we see firsthand this balance of both acceptance (accepting your past and precipitating factors, as well as any maintaining factors that are out of your control) and change (identifying ways in which you can change your maintaining factors). The rest of this chapter will focus specifically on acceptance, and the process of change will be discussed throughout the remainder of this book.

Practicing Acceptance

At the end of Kate's essay, she described some ways in which she is practicing acceptance. It's relevant to think about ways in which you can help yourself accept the items you listed as precipitating and maintaining factors. While acceptance is key for all factors, it is particularly relevant for the items that are solely precipitating factors, as these are experiences from the past and cannot be changed. While some may be easy to accept (*I can't change my genetics, so I just have to accept that these were cards I was dealt.*), others may be more difficult (*How do I accept my past trauma?*).

Below are some DBT-based ways to practice acceptance (Linehan 1993). While you can begin the process of acceptance on your own by identifying how you want to approach each of your precipitating factors and by trying out different ideas, involving your psychotherapist and other team members will be beneficial in helping you to work through acceptance fully. They know your individual situation and can help guide you in practicing acceptance. It is not likely that you will read about these three modes of acceptance and immediately be able to do them. Acceptance is a process, and this process is often best facilitated through psychotherapy, working on it collaboratively with your psychotherapist.

Radical Acceptance

Kate described radical acceptance when she wrote, "I've learned that I can't change my past, and I realize that I need to stop fighting with the reality of my past. I also can't change the fact that my mom won't participate in my treatment." When you practice radical acceptance, you choose to accept your precipitating factors completely and fully. This means you are no longer fighting the reality of what happened. For example, rather than being angry that your parents put so much pressure on you as a child, you can radically accept this by saying—and truly believing, "Those were the cards I was dealt. I am ready to move on from that and make the changes I need to make in myself and in my life to do so." Radical acceptance does not mean that you agree with what happened or think that what happened is okay. Rather, it means you accept reality for what it is. In the space below, describe an instance in which you could apply radical acceptance in your life.

_____

_____

_____

Validation

Validation is the process of acknowledging and accepting your own or someone else's experience as understandable and valid. This does not necessarily mean that you agree with what you or another person is thinking, feeling, or doing. Rather, you are able to see how your or another's experience makes sense. To practice self-validation, you may choose to recognize, admit, and accept your feelings and thoughts in the moment. For example, *I'm feeling anxious and am body-conscious, and that is okay because that is where I am currently. I am allowed to have feelings and thoughts about my body. I have an eating disorder, so it makes sense that these feelings are present.* Kate provided a great example of self-validation when she wrote, "I'm quite angry with my mom for all of this, but rather than trying to stop my anger, I'm working on acknowledging and accepting these feelings." What are two statements you can tell yourself that are self-validating?

1. _____

_____

_____

2. _____

_____

_____

You can also seek validation of your experiences from others, such as your treatment team members and support system. Validation from others requires taking some potentially scary steps of being open, honest, and vulnerable in sharing what you are thinking, feeling, and doing. If you do not share your experiences, others do not have the opportunity to provide you with validation. You may also have to tell others that you need validation, as it is common for others to respond with reassurance, attempts to challenge your thinking, or problem-solving ideas. In the space below, name one person with whom you can be open, honest, and vulnerable? What are some validating statements that could be helpful from this person?

_____

_____

_____

Forgiveness

You may also need to work toward forgiving yourself or others who have had a role in the development of your eating disorder. For example, *I'm angry at myself for succumbing to the peer pressure to try purging; however, I need to forgive myself and show myself compassion. Many people are affected by peer pressure, and having done this does not make me a bad person.* Practicing forgiveness can be hard and can take time. Start small, forgiving yourself and others for things that feel natural and easy. You can also foster forgiveness by recognizing and being grateful for what your or others' actions have taught you. It can also be helpful to put yourself in the shoes of others to help you empathize with them, helping you to better understand and relate to what they have been through or decisions they have made. Empathy for both yourself and others is a key component for forgiveness. What are three things you can forgive yourself for in this moment?

1. _____

2. _____

3. _____

My Reflections on Acceptance

Using the ideas above for practicing acceptance, and combining them with your own ideas on how to implement and practice acceptance, write about which modes of acceptance you identify with most and which you feel will most help you in your recovery. How might you go about practicing acceptance with each of your precipitating and maintaining factors?

_____

_____

_____

Journaling Pages

In this chapter, we discussed precipitating and maintaining factors related to eating disorders, the usefulness in understanding why your eating disorder developed, ways to accept your past and present circumstances, and the role of acceptance as a means of facilitating change. In the beginning of the chapter, Kate shared her narrative of her understanding of her eating disorder. Use the space below to write your story. Write about how you got to where you are now in your life, your eating disorder, and your recovery. Similar to Kate's experience, many people find the process of making sense of and telling their story—whether in a private journal, to a psychotherapist, or in a group setting—to be relieving and therapeutic.

Chapter 5

Letting Go of Your Eating Disorder

Incredible change happens in your life when you decide to take control of what you do have power over instead of craving control over what you don't.

—Steve Maraboli

Meet Sophie

Sophie has been seeing an outpatient team since being discharged from her local hospital three months ago, where she had been admitted for medical stabilization. Still trying to figure out what recovery means for her, she struggles with her commitment to improving her physical and mental well-being. She feels stuck between wanting to live a life she enjoys and fearing giving up control over her eating behaviors and weight. As a result, she continues to weigh herself daily, counts calories religiously, and avoids foods that she does not prepare herself. In an effort to avoid feeling like a failure—and out of fear of disappointing her treatment team—she is not forthcoming about her struggle to give up these behaviors. She recognizes that her ambivalence and hiding her difficulties are impeding her ability to move forward with recovery. However, Sophie's fear of getting better feels paralyzing, as "getting better" for her not only means improved health and living a meaningful life but also gaining a significant amount of weight, giving up her only sense of identity, losing a means of coping with difficult emotions, and being uncomfortably vulnerable.

The Difficulty in Letting Go

As mentioned in chapter 4, both acceptance and change are relevant components for recovery from anorexia. One change that needs to occur is letting go of your eating disorder. As discussed, your eating disorder likely has filled a void and has served one or more purposes in your life (e.g., a means of communication, control, and coping). It is also familiar and, in a way, comfortable, at least compared to the idea of what may happen if you recover, which is often scary, unfamiliar territory. This makes fully letting go of your eating disordered thoughts, behaviors, and attitudes potentially difficult. However, in order to continue with your recovery and fully commit to a life without an eating disorder, letting go completely, even of the seemingly most insignificant habits, is important.

Relinquishing Control over Your Eating Disorder

In order to progress in your recovery, you need to relinquish control over your eating disorder. You need to give up eating disordered goals, behaviors, and attitudes. But, as illustrated in Sophie's case, this is easier said than done. Despite Sophie's desire for recovery, her fear of what recovery would look like makes recovery difficult to maintain. Like Sophie, you may also be facing this challenge. If giving up your eating disorder were as easy as throwing it in the garbage and never looking back, recovery would be simple, and this book would not be needed. Giving up your eating disordered thoughts, behaviors, and attitudes is a process, and this process is different for everyone.

Identifying the parts of your eating disorder you need to give up control over is just the first step. Sophie's story listed several areas that she is struggling to give up control over, including weighing herself daily, counting calories, avoiding certain foods, and keeping information from her treatment team. Below is a list of behaviors that many people need to change or give up in their recovery. Circle or highlight the ones you identify as challenges. Remember that everyone's recovery is different. Not all of them will apply to your recovery, as some of these behaviors may not have been a problem area in your eating disorder, or you have successfully begun to overcome them already.

- Restricting your food or caloric intake

- Bingeing or purging

- Overexercising

- Abusing laxatives or diuretics

- Weighing yourself obsessively, compulsively, too frequently, or at all, depending on what is recommended by your treatment providers

- Counting calories; reading nutrition labels

- Food rituals (cutting food up into tiny pieces, eating foods in a certain order, chewing and spitting, or separating your food)

- Avoiding certain foods; only eating "safe" foods and avoiding foods that you fear or cause anxiety; choosing fat-free, reduced-fat, or low-calorie options

- Body checking (measuring body parts, pinching parts of your body in the mirror, standing at certain angles to see bones or gaps as reassurance for thinness, or taking pictures of yourself in order to compare your body at different weights)

- Holding onto "sick clothes" (clothes that fit you at unhealthy weights)

- Relying on supplements for nutrition rather than food

- Isolating yourself socially, perhaps to avoid situations with food

- Eating based on your current emotions, weight, or how your clothes fit, rather than based on hunger or fullness cues or your meal plan

- Keeping secrets about your behaviors from your treatment team

What are some other parts of your eating disorder that need improvement? Add these ideas here.

- _____

- _____

- _____

- _____

- _____

Like Sophie, you may face times of ambivalence that can either keep you static or lead you away from recovery. As her story described, merely recognizing how you need to let go of your eating disorder does not necessarily indicate change. Therefore, in addition to behaviorally letting go of your eating disorder by challenging the behaviors you identified above, you need to also change the way you think. There are various ways to help make this shift in your thoughts. Try some of the following strategies and observe if they help you over time. Some of them may be more helpful for you than others (and some might not help much at all), and none of them will likely have an immediate effect on your thinking. Use them multiple times a day, particularly when faced with challenges in your recovery, and see where they take you.

Radical Acceptance

Radical acceptance, as described in the previous chapter, is a DBT-based therapy in which you accept life as it is rather than resisting what you cannot change (Linehan 1993). Instead of mentally fighting what is unfair, stressful, or difficult in your life, you embrace the fact that "it is what it is." You do not have to agree with or like your current situation to radically accept it. Let's work through some examples in your life where radical acceptance may be applicable and necessary, as Sophie has done.

What is a difficult, stressful, or unfair situation you are experiencing?

Having to gain weight.

What makes this situation feel difficult, stressful, or unfair?

I know I will feel super uncomfortable at a higher weight. I'm scared I will become overweight or obese. It makes me anxious to think about giving up counting calories and eating more types of foods.

What aspects of this situation am I unable to change (or if I changed them, I would be moving away from recovery)?

I can't recover without gaining weight. I can't change the weight at which my body is at its healthiest. I can't hold on to eating disordered behaviors and gain weight at the same time, so I have to work on giving them up.

What can I tell myself to help me accept these things that cannot change in this moment?

I have to gain and maintain this weight. I don't agree with it. It makes me feel uncomfortable and angry, but it is what it is. I cannot change that this is the weight at which my body is healthiest.

Now think of your own difficult, stressful, or unfair situation and complete the exercise below. This exercise is also available at http://www.newharbinger.com/39348.

> **What is a difficult, stressful, or unfair situation you are experiencing?**

> **What makes this situation feel difficult, stressful, or unfair?**

> **What aspects of this situation am I unable to change (or if I changed them, I would be moving away from recovery)?**

> **What can I tell myself to help me accept these things that cannot change in this moment?**

Surrender to the Process

Many people find it helpful to view themselves as surrendering to the process of recovery. To surrender to the process, you give up control and put complete trust in your treatment team and your recovery. You remind yourself every day that while it is painful in the moment, the difficult emotions will pass. You maintain hope that going through the motions of recovery will become more natural with time and will be worth it in the end.

For Sophie, a step toward surrendering toward the process of recovery could be giving her scale to a friend or her dietitian, resisting the urges to buy a new one, and reminding herself that the discomfort of not knowing her weight each day will pass and get easier—and that it is necessary in order for her to live a full and meaningful life. What are some parts of recovery that you are struggling to accept as part of the process? What ways could you practice surrendering to the process of recovery?

_____

_____

_____

_____

_____

Develop Trust

Although a difficult task for many individuals with anorexia, fully trusting your treatment team can be a liberating psychological shift. Before we continue talking about trust, let's take a moment to evaluate your trust with your treatment team right now. On a scale of 0 to 10, with 0 indicating no trust at all and 10 indicating complete trust, how much do you trust your treatment team members?

Psychotherapist: _____

Dietitian: _____

Psychiatrist: _____

Primary care physician: _____

Trust is not an easy feat, and it depends on various factors—how long you have worked with team members, the strength and nature of the relationships you have with them, and how much you are able to trust others based on your personal history. What are some factors that impact your ability to trust your treatment team?

_____

_____

_____

_____

Trusting your treatment team's recommendations in the recovery process is important. Without that trust, you are more likely to listen to your eating disordered thoughts. Developing trust takes time and effort on both sides of the relationship. Remember that your treatment team is serving as the voice to counteract your eating disorder. They have your best interest in mind and are able to assess your situation more objectively than you can. If you are finding it difficult to trust your team members, talk about it with them. Try to decide if the mistrust is deserved or misplaced. In most cases, your difficulty with trusting your team will be related to fear of letting go of your eating disorder or to past events in your experience, in which trusting others had negative consequences. Why do you not trust your treatment team members? Is it due to interactions you have had with them—things they've done? Is your difficulty related to fully letting go of your eating disorder? What past experiences related to trust impact your trust of your treatment team? What are some things your treatment team members can do to help earn your trust? Are there some issues you can discuss with them that may help build trust between you and them? If so, what are they? Use the space below to reflect on these questions.

_____

_____

_____

_____

_____

Unfortunately, in some cases your treatment team may truly not be meeting your needs for recovery. Hopefully, your treatment team members are competently educated on eating disorders, but this cannot be assumed. If you feel your treatment team's recommendations are not in your best interest, try to talk with them about your concerns and, if need be, seek out a second opinion or a new treatment team.

Find a Mantra

You may find it helpful to find or develop a mantra that you repeat to yourself in difficult times. *Mantras*—motivational phrases—are concise reminders that help you move forward in your recovery. To shift your mind-set and free yourself psychologically from your eating disorder, this mantra should be related to letting go of unhealthy behaviors and thoughts that do not serve you. For example:

- Letting go gives us freedom, and freedom is the only condition for happiness. (Thich Nhat Hanh)

- Accept what is, let go of what was, and have faith in what will be. (Sonia Ricotti)

- We either make ourselves miserable, or we make ourselves strong. The amount of work is the same. (Carlos Castaneda)

Find a mantra that is meaningful and resonates with you, and repeat it as often as necessary. What are some mantras that you think may be helpful for you? Write your ideas below.

_____

_____

_____

_____

_____

Create a Vision Board

Vision boards are pictorial, rather than verbal, reminders to help motivate you to push through tough times and continue with recovery-oriented choices, even when resorting back to eating disordered behaviors may seem easier. Find a picture or create a collage that represents what recovery means to you. This may include pictures that remind you to relax, pictures of loved ones, or pictures of things that you value more than your eating disorder (further discussion on values will be presented in chapter 6). What are some ideas of visual reminders that you can include in your vision board?

- _____
- _____
- _____
- _____
- _____

Fake It Until You Make It

It may seem paradoxical, but it can help to fake it. "Fake it until you make it" may be a common phrase, but it can really work. The idea is that if you keep faking it, your actions and thoughts will eventually become internalized and natural for you. In the case of recovery from anorexia, "faking it" could mean consciously making behavioral choices that are in line with your recovery—regardless of how you actually feel about recovery in that moment. "Faking it" could also mean repeatedly telling yourself positive statements (*I am beautiful. I accept my body. I can eat this even though I do not feel hungry. My body and mind need this food.*) whether or not you believe them in that moment. Identify what you need to fake, and do just that, trusting that eventually you will not be faking these behaviors and thoughts, but doing them because you want to or you believe in them. Can you think of thoughts or behaviors that you could fake to help you in your recovery? See Sophie's answers for some guidance and write your ideas below.

Thoughts	Behaviors
I am more than my eating disorder. *Any time I weigh myself, I can tell myself, "This number does not tell me my self-worth."*	*I can go through the motions of eating enough despite how hungry or full I am.* *I will go to each of my appointments even if I'm too tired or want to avoid them.*

Try It Out

Some individuals find comfort and peace of mind in viewing their recovery as a trial run. That is, you are going to "try out" recovery and give it your all for a definitive amount of time, such as one year. If, at the end of the year, you want to stop fighting for recovery, you can. This is not to say you have the intention of ever going back to your eating disorder. Instead, it gives you an "out" and an end point if things get too hard. You can modify this trial run to fit your needs; some people may need to take it day by day ("I'm going to choose recovery today, and if I want to go back to my eating disordered behaviors tomorrow, I can."), while for others, end points of several months or a year are enough to get them through the tough times when they want to hold on to their eating disorder. Psychologically, this helps make recovery—which can feel like an ominous and never-ending battle—more manageable, and it can take some pressure off. Reminding yourself that you have a limited amount of time that you have committed to recovery (a commitment that can be renewed indefinitely at the end of the previous one) helps delay your urges to act on your eating disorder.

Try putting this technique into practice by creating a contract with yourself. This contract can be continuously revised, and it can be done either in a written format or in your mind. Fill in this sample contract to help you commit to "trying it out" in recovery.

I, _____, commit to choosing recovery for _____.
          (name)   (amount of time)

For this amount of time, I will not engage in the following eating disordered behaviors:

_____

_____

_____

I will reevaluate my commitment to recovery on _____.
                                                                    (date)

Signed,

_____
          (your signature)

This technique also helps to give you a sense of control. No one is taking your eating disorder away from you. You are choosing to commit to recovery, and you can choose to relapse in the future. Remember that you are really good at losing weight and having an eating disorder. Let's try something new and be really good at recovery! The longer you stay in recovery and are mindful of the benefits of it, the less you will need to find comfort in reminding yourself that you have the ability to relapse. The motivation and your ability to continue to let go of your eating disordered mind-set and behaviors will become more internal, natural, and comfortable as time passes.

Create a Pros and Cons List

You may find it helpful to create a list of the positives and the negatives for continuing in recovery. There will be some negatives, some cons—after all, if you were not getting something positive out of your eating disorder, you would not have difficulty with letting it go. For example, a pro may be being able to go out to eat with friends without obsessing about what you are going to order. A con might be gaining weight, like in the case of Sophie. We encourage you to acknowledge the cons of letting go of your eating disorder, but focus on the pros. It is helpful to write down the pros and keep the list somewhere you can easily look at it. Use these reasons as your motivation and reminder of why you are fighting to let go of your eating disorder. What are the pros and cons of recovery for you? See Sophie's responses and write your ideas below.

Pros of Recovery	Cons of Recovery
Being able to be honest	Losing a coping mechanism
Having meaningful relationships	Losing a part of my identity
Not being cold all the time	Feeling uncomfortable during weight gain

Do the Opposite

Sometimes a tough-love approach with yourself is necessary and helpful. While self-compassion is important in accepting yourself and your struggles, there are times when saying to yourself *Just do it. Whatever my eating disorder's voice wants me to do, I just need to suck it up and do the opposite of that!* is more effective. As with several of the other techniques above, behavioral changes often translate into cognitive changes over time. Thus, by consciously and deliberately doing the opposite of what your eating disorder is telling you to do (restrict, berate yourself in front of a mirror, or isolate yourself from friends), you prove to yourself—over and over—that doing the opposite is not going to lead to a catastrophic result. And, as with all of the suggestions above, over time, your thoughts and attitude will shift to being more oriented toward recovery. Can you think of examples of when doing the opposite would be helpful for your recovery? Try to differentiate between observable behaviors (behaviors that you or others can see, such as restricting, purging, exercising, bingeing, or taking laxatives), mental behaviors (behaviors that only you know are going on in your head, such as keeping track of your calories for the day or negative self-talk), and interpersonal behaviors (behaviors that involve your relationships with others, such as lying about your struggles or isolating yourself from friends). Review Sophie's examples immediately below and then complete the activity on the following page to begin brainstorming ways you can do the opposite of what your eating disorder is telling you to do.

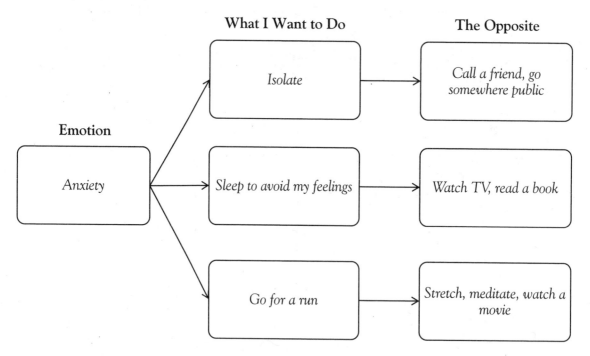

Now complete the activity using examples from your own life. This exercise is also available at http://www.newharbinger.com/39348.

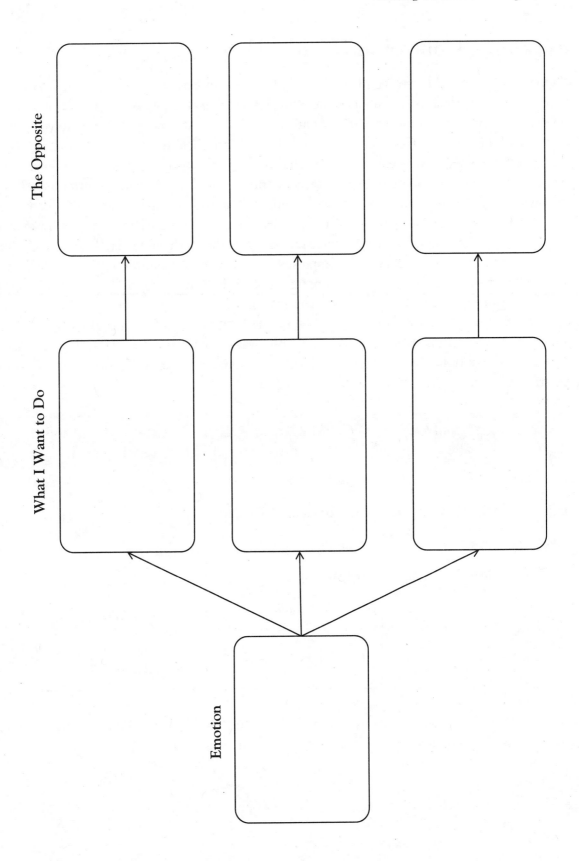

Regaining Control in Healthy Ways

Giving up control and letting go of your eating disorder can leave you feeling immensely out of control (which is why it is so difficult to actually do). Having control over your life is important regardless of whether you have a history of an eating disorder. It is normal for you to want a say in how your life unfolds. However, there are healthy and unhealthy means of control. Healthy control is taking charge of areas of your life that you are able to change and that enhance your overall well-being—and doing so in a balanced manner. Examples of healthy control include following your meal plan, setting appropriate boundaries with others, and achieving life goals. On the other hand, unhealthy control is trying to control something that is unchangeable or outside of your control. For example, you may make changes that diminish your overall well-being, often in a way that is obsessive, excessive, or compulsive. Examples of unhealthy control include forcing your body to be at a weight lower than its natural state, criticizing or controlling what others eat, and putting stringent rules on your and others' behaviors.

Let's take some time to distinguish between what you can control in a healthy manner, what you need to give up controlling (i.e., the unhealthy ways you are asserting control), and what is beyond your control. Use Sophie's chart below as guidance as you reflect on your own experiences.

What can I control?	What do I need to give up controlling?	What is beyond my control?
My actions and behaviors	My food intake	My body's natural, healthy weight
Being authentic and vulnerable	Negative emotions	Whether others' like or dislike me
Challenging myself	My weight	Others' actions
Being honest with others and myself	Trying to be perfect	My personality
Reaching out when I need support	Others' food intake	Whatever caused me to develop an eating disorder

Complete the following chart as you reflect on what you can control in a healthy manner, what you need to give up controlling, and what is beyond your control.

What can I control?	What do I need to give up controlling?	What is beyond my control?

The next step is to focus on the first column—things you can (healthily) control in your life. Remember that healthy control keeps your overall well-being at the forefront of your decisions and emphasizes moderation in your actions. How do you think you can begin to take control of these things? What are some steps you can take in the short and long term? See Sophie's responses on the next page as an example, and then write your own ideas. It also would be fruitful to discuss and process this idea of letting go of your eating disorder and regaining control in healthy ways with your psychotherapist, as it is likely to be a difficult task both behaviorally and mentally. And, as you reflect and brainstorm, it may be useful to keep the Serenity Prayer in mind:

Grant me the serenity to accept the things I cannot change, the courage to change the things I can, and the wisdom to know the difference.

Sophie's Reflections on Control

The areas of my life I can control include my actions and behaviors, being authentic and vulnerable, challenging myself, being honest with others and myself, and reaching out when I need support. I think the biggest change I can and need to make is to be honest with my treatment team. By being honest, I will be focusing on all five areas I have identified as areas of my life that I can control. I think it is a reasonable first step in taking control of myself in a healthy way. I know I'm not ready to be 100 percent open with everyone in my life, and I don't think that would be particularly helpful at this moment. However, I can begin with being truthful with myself and with my psychotherapist.

Your Reflections on Control

_____

_____

_____

_____

_____

Grieving the Loss of Your Eating Disorder

Giving up your eating disorder often involves a grieving process. Your eating disorder has most likely become part of your identity and a primary means of coping with stress and painful emotions. Also, making the mental and behavioral shifts from being "someone with anorexia" to "someone in recovery" and eventually to "someone who recovered" can feel unfamiliar and uncomfortable. It is common to experience feelings of fear, guilt, shame, anger, longing, and sadness as you progress through recovery, particularly in times of stress or in situations that would typically trigger the use of eating disordered behaviors and thoughts.

Much of this chapter has aimed to help you focus on the positive aspects of recovering from anorexia. However, it would be dismissive and invalidating of your experience to not take time to acknowledge the negative aspects of being in recovery—of not having an eating disorder. These negative aspects are the parts you grieve, and it is important to acknowledge, validate, and allow yourself room to experience your emotions related to the grieving process.

Sophie identified several areas of grief that she will have to overcome: gaining a significant amount of weight, giving up her only sense of identity, losing a means of coping with difficult emotions, and being uncomfortably vulnerable. As a starting point for you and your psychotherapist to address and process your grief, consider this question: What does it mean for you to not have an eating disorder? Check all the responses that apply to you. Then, on the next page, answer the questions.

——— Giving up a way of coping with my emotions

——— Not being able to numb my emotions anymore

——— Gaining weight and likely feeling uncomfortable in my body

——— Losing a main part of myself or my identity

——— Losing others' care for me

——— Feeling out of control

——— Feeling like I failed

——— Not knowing where I will be able to cultivate a sense of self-worth or accomplishment

——— Fear of losing relationships with those who will no longer have to worry about me

——— Feeling vulnerable and uncomfortable

——— Having to face and deal with my problems and responsibilities

——— Going against what feels natural for me

——— Losing my main distraction from difficult things in life

——— Others commenting on my changing body and eating habits

——— Fear that others will expect too much of me

——— Losing the sense of safety I feel with my eating disorder

——— Having to face and manage feeling angry, jealous, lonely, sad, or anxious

What else does it mean to you to no longer have an eating disorder?

_____

_____

_____

_____

_____

What does gaining weight or maintaining a healthy weight mean for you and your life?

_____

_____

_____

_____

_____

What does not being "the sick one" mean?

_____

_____

_____

_____

What will you miss or what do you already miss about your eating disorder at times, now that you are in recovery?

_____

_____

_____

_____

_____

Journaling Pages

In this chapter, we discussed letting go of eating disordered behaviors and attitudes and various ways to shift your thoughts and attitudes toward your eating disorder. We also explored healthy versus unhealthy control and the process of grief that can be present as you move further into recovery. What emotions and thoughts came up for you as you completed this chapter? Maybe you noticed yourself feeling empowered by some of the information presented. Or perhaps you noticed your mind resisting some of the ideas (perhaps thinking, *These will never work*). Write down your reactions, whatever they may be, below. Notice them without judging them. There is no right or wrong way to feel about the material. Bring your thoughts to your psychotherapist in order to allow you to process them further.

_____

_____

_____

_____

_____

_____

_____

_____

_____

_____

_____

_____

_____

_____

Chapter 6

Building Healthy Life Goals

The goal you set must be challenging. At the same time, it should be realistic and attainable, not impossible to reach. It should be challenging enough to make you stretch, but not so far that you break.

—Rick Hansen

Meet Sari

Sari is preparing to transition from inpatient treatment to intensive outpatient treatment for her eating disorder. While she has made some progress in her recovery during her inpatient stay, she feels overwhelmed at the amount of work she will need to do as she moves to a lower level of care in order to continue improving her health and overall well-being. She told her therapist as she left the hospital, "What if I can't do it? The thought of eating enough to gain weight all on my own, not exercising it all off, going back to work plus groups and therapy in the evenings, and having to try to be 'normal' for my family just all feels like too much to do at once. Especially without my eating disorder to help me cope with the stress. I have no idea how I'm going to ever fully recovery. I mean—I have to get better for my family, but what if I don't really want to?" With wavering motivation and ambivalence about wanting to recover, she fears that gaining the amount of weight her providers are recommending, abstaining from eating disordered behaviors, and integrating fully back into her job and family life may be unattainable goals.

Goals in Recovery

As part of your recovery process, it is important to replace your old eating disordered goals with healthy life, recovery-oriented goals. This includes goals regarding your weight, food intake, and exercise habits, as well as healthy goals for life outside of your eating disorder—your education, career, relationships, and hobbies. In chapter 5, you took some time to reflect on challenges that you are still facing in recovery and aspects of your eating disorder that you are having difficulty letting go of. We discussed how letting go of controlling things through your eating disorder can be made easier as you gain control in healthy, adaptive ways in your life. Being realistic and successful in this process of regaining control is challenging but important, and healthy goal setting is a valuable skill that can aid you in your journey.

What Are Your Values?

If implementing the changes you need to make were as easy as thinking *Okay, I won't weigh myself, purge, count calories, and overexercise anymore*, recovery from anorexia would not take an average of five years (American Psychiatric Association 2013). So, rather than making a list of behaviors you must stop and then painfully and slowly crossing them off your list—which would not likely lead to a lasting recovery—let's take a different approach. Instead of setting negative goals (*stop this, eliminate that*), let's create positive goals that add healthy behaviors and attitudes to your life. But in order to set the best and most effective positive goals, let's take a step back to examine what motivates the goals we set for ourselves.

Similar to dialectical behavior therapy (Linehan 1993), acceptance and commitment therapy (ACT) is a commonly used and evidence-based treatment for individuals with eating disorders (e.g., Berman, Boutelle, and Crow 2009; Juarascio et al. 2013; Sandoz, Wilson, and DuFrene 2010). In ACT, you are encouraged to identify what you value in yourself, others, and the world. Then you use these values to guide your actions. Your values give you purpose, and they can be your reasons to go against your typical eating disordered thoughts and behaviors.

Values are what we want from ourselves and in life; they are what we stand for (Hayes, Strosahl, and Wilson 2012). Our values motivate us and give us guidance and direction in order to live a meaningful life. Values are *not* goals, desires, morals, needs, or feelings. Rather, values are ongoing (not finite, like goals), they come from within (not something we get from others, like desires or needs), and they express what matters most to us (not things we view as good or bad, like morals). Living and acting in line with our values helps us to lead meaningful lives. Living a meaningful life helps us feel authentic, purposeful, and worthwhile in our time and efforts (Hayes, Strosahl, and Wilson 2012).

To identify your values, ask yourself questions such as *What do I want to stand for in life? How do I want to behave and interact with myself, others, and the world? What is most important to me?* It also may be helpful to think about the following categories, or domains, in which your values likely fall: family; intimate relationships; friendships; employment; education and personal development; recreation, fun, and leisure; spirituality; community life; environment and nature; health and body (Hayes, Strosahl, and Wilson 2012). Write your answers to the questions below using these ten categories as overarching topics or areas to consider. Not every domain will be a high priority for you; some will be more important than others. Take your time and try to complete the exercise for each domain. Your thoughts do not need to be clear and concise—and they might not sound like values just yet; we will get there. Sari completed the exercise below to begin exploring her values as a means of setting healthy and attainable goals for herself. Her answers can serve as examples of how someone approaches the questions. Take your time to reflect on each of these domains, as the work on your values in this chapter will be useful in subsequent chapters.

Family: What do I want to stand for in terms of family? How do I define family? How do I want to behave and interact with my family? What is most important to me in terms of family?

Sari: *I really want to be a good mom to my children and a good partner to my husband. It is important for me to regain my physical and mental health in order to be able to be there for my family.*

You: _____

_____

_____

Intimate Relationships: What do I want to stand for in my intimate relationships? What qualities do I want to exhibit in my intimate relationships? How do I want to behave and interact with myself and others when it comes to intimate relationships? What is most important to me in my intimate relationships?

Sari: *Because of my eating disorder, I have not wanted to be intimate with my husband, and I have been significantly more irritable with him. This has definitely taken a toll on our marriage. Our relationship is important to me, but I have not been able to show that since getting sick.*

You: _____

_____

_____

Friendships: What do I want to stand for in my friendships? What qualities do I want to exhibit in my friendships? How do I want to behave and interact with myself and others when it comes to friendships? What is most important to me in my friendships?

Sari: *I used to be very social, but I don't have many friends right now. I want to be confident in myself so that I feel comfortable in social situations. It's important for me to reestablish and maintain a social network.*

You: _____

_____

_____

Employment: What do I want to stand for in terms of employment? How do I want to behave and interact with myself, others, and the world within this domain? What qualities do I want to inhabit as an employee or employer? What is most important to me in terms of employment?

Sari: *My passion in life is teaching. I want to create a classroom environment that is fun and interactive for the kids, and I want to share my love of learning with my students.*

You: _____

_____

_____

Education and Personal Development: What do I want to stand for in terms of my education and personal development? What do I want personal development to look like for me? How do I want to behave and interact with myself, others, and the world within this domain? What is most important to me when it comes to education and personal development?

Sari: *Personal growth and learning are very important to me. I want to be healthy enough to concentrate and commit to exploring something new.*

You: _____

_____

_____

Recreation, Fun, and Leisure: What do I want to stand for within this domain? How do I want to engage in life in terms of recreation, fun, and leisure? How do I want to behave and interact with myself, others, and the world within this domain? What do I consider recreation, fun, or leisure? What is most important to me when it comes to recreation, fun, and leisure?

Sari: *I used to enjoy playing with my kids, going to the movies with my husband, and planning social events with my friends. Since my eating disorder began, I have lost touch with the pleasure each of these things provided me. I want to reconnect with those activities, and I want to be able to enjoy downtime.*

You: _____

_____

_____

Spirituality: What do I want to stand for in terms of spirituality? What does spirituality mean to me? How do I want to behave and interact with myself, others, and the world when it comes to spirituality? What is most important to me within this domain?

Sari: *I don't know what I stand for in this domain. I'm not religious, but I would like to explore my beliefs and feel connected to something greater than me. I'm not sure how to navigate this area of my life at this time.*

You: _____

_____

_____

Community Life: What are my communities (e.g., religious communities, neighborhood communities, cultural communities)? What do I want to stand for within my community? How do I want to behave and interact with myself, others, and the world when it comes to community life? What is most important to me in terms of community?

Sari: *I want to serve my community, especially those less fortunate than me.*

You: _____

_____

_____

Environment and Nature: In what ways are nature and the environment important to me? What do I want to stand for within this domain? How do I want to behave and interact with myself, others, and the world in terms of the environment and nature? What is most important to me within this domain?

Sari: *It is important for me to spend time outside. I love hiking and going to the beach.*

You: _____

_____

_____

Health and Body: What do I want to stand for in terms of health and my body? How do I want to behave and interact with myself, others, and the world with regard to health? What is most important to me within this domain?

Sari: *I want to be healthy, physically and mentally, so I can enjoy my life in the ways I have described above. I want to recover from my eating disorder.*

You: _____

_____

_____

Now, reread your thoughts and reflect on the themes that have emerged. It may be useful to elicit feedback from your psychotherapist, as he or she is trained in identifying patterns and themes and can help you to become aware of them and their meaning. Sometimes it is hard to put language to your values. On the opposite page is a list of values to help you get started. You likely identify with each of these on some level—but remember that the purpose of this exercise is to find your top values, so choose five to seven values that are most important to you.

Values List

Acceptance	Courage	Humility	Perseverance
Accomplishment	Creativity	Humor	Pleasure
Accountability	Dependability	Independence	Popularity
Achievement	Determination	Individuality	Power
Adaptability	Dignity	Inspiration	Rationality
Adventure	Direction	Integrity	Relaxation
Affection	Discipline	Intelligence	Reliability
Altruism	Discovery	Intimacy	Resilience
Ambition	Education	Introspection	Respect
Appreciation	Efficiency	Joy	Responsibility
Approval	Empathy	Justice	Selflessness
Assertiveness	Energy	Kindness	Self-reliance
Attractiveness	Enthusiasm	Knowledge	Self-respect
Awareness	Exploration	Leadership	Serenity
Balance	Fairness	Learning	Service
Beauty	Faith	Logic	Sexuality
Benevolence	Family	Love	Simplicity
Bravery	Fidelity	Loyalty	Sincerity
Calmness	Flexibility	Mastery	Skillfulness
Challenge	Fortitude	Maturity	Spirituality
Change	Freedom	Modesty	Spontaneity
Comfort	Friendship	Motivation	Stability
Community	Fun	Noncomformity	Strength
Compassion	Generosity	Openness	Success
Competence	Gratitude	Optimism	Trust
Confidence	Growth	Order	Understanding
Conformity	Health	Originality	Variety
Connection	Helpfulness	Patience	Warmth
Contentment	Honesty	Passion	Wealth
Contribution	Hopefulness	Peace	Wisdom

Values Cards

Another helpful and effective way to determine your values is by creating and using values cards. Write the values above on index cards—one value per card—or go to casaa.unm.edu/inst /Personal Values Card Sort.pdf for a free set of values cards (Miller et al. 2001) to cut out. Once you have your cards ready, complete the following steps:

1. On first instinct, place each card in one of three piles: Not Important to Me, Important to Me, and Very Important to Me.

2. Discard the Not Important to Me and Important to Me piles.

3. Take the Very Important to Me pile and place each card in one of two piles: Things I Feel I Should Value and Things I Truly Value.

4. Then take the Things I Truly Value and separate them into one of two piles: Important to Me and Very Important to Me.

5. Take the remaining Very Important to Me cards and put them in order from most important to least.

6. Pick up the first five to seven cards, the ones that are most important to you. These are your values! Write them below.

_____

_____

_____

_____

_____

_____

_____

Setting Values-Based SMART Goals

Now that you have identified your values, you are ready to use them to set intentions and goals for yourself and your recovery. In ACT, you are encouraged to use your values as guidance and as a focal point when setting goals for yourself (Harris 2008). Thus, your goals will reflect your values and will help you to live in accordance with those values. Let's focus on one value at a time. Just as Sari has done in the diagram below, write one of your values in the space on the left and then identify which of the ten domains (from earlier in this chapter) may require improvement or change in order for you to create a meaningful life. This diagram is also available at http://www.newharbinger.com/39348. As a reminder, the ten domains are family; intimate relationships; friendships; employment; education and personal development; recreation, fun, and leisure; spirituality; community life; environment and nature; and health and body.

Sari: *I'm going to choose to focus on my most important value: connection. In order for me to live more in line with this value, I need to address the following domains in my life: family, friendships, intimate relationships, employment, and community life.*

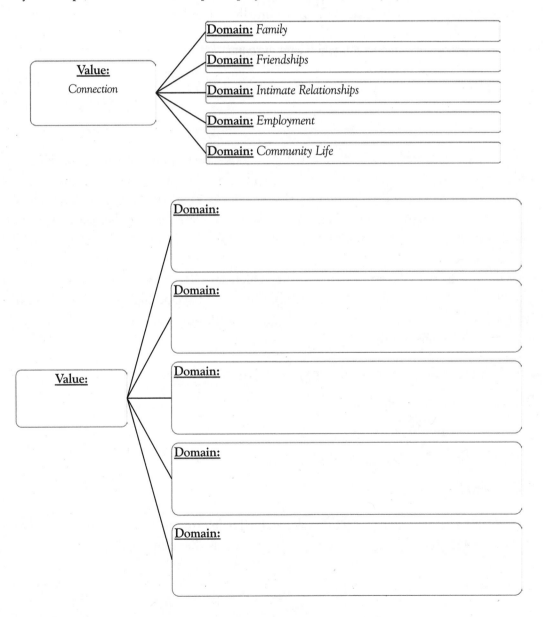

Using your identified value and domains, take a moment to think about and respond to the following questions to begin the process of setting a values-based SMART goal. Sari's answers are used here as examples. Use the spaces below to write your own responses.

For what value and domain do I want to set goals?

Sari: *I will focus on connection with my family.*

You: _____

_____

What is one goal that I can set to help me improve my life related to this value and domain?

Sari: *I can spend more quality time with my kids and husband.*

You: _____

_____

Sari's goal seems reasonable and concrete, but if we look closer, there are many questions that have not been answered: What does she mean by "quality time"? How much is *more* quality time? When and where will she spend more quality time with her kids and husband? How will she know when she has achieved her goal? Perhaps the goal you stated above also leaves you with some of these questions. To help us modify Sari's and your goals, we can use the format provided by SMART goals.

The SMART goal method ensures that your goal is specific, measurable, attainable and adaptive, realistic, and time-sensitive (Doran 1981). Once you have addressed each of these five aspects, you will have a solid goal that you can begin to work on achieving. Let's take a deeper look at what SMART goals stands for.

S = *Specific*. With specific goals, you can typically answer the following questions:

- What do I want to accomplish?
- Why am I setting this goal?
- Who is involved in my attainment of this goal?
- Where will I achieve this goal?

M = *Measurable*. Measurable goals have tangible, quantifiable criteria for determining your progress. With measurable goals, you can answer questions such as the following:

- How much?

- How many?
- How will I know when it is accomplished?

A = *Attainable and Adaptive.* Attainable goals are neither extreme nor out of reach. An adaptive goal serves a positive purpose in your life and recovery and helps you head in the direction of improving your quality of life. Thus with an attainable and adaptive goal, you should be able to answer the following questions:

- How can this goal be accomplished? What steps are required?
- What limitations or constraints will I need to overcome?
- How is this goal going to serve me on my path toward recovery?

R = *Realistic.* Realistic goals are reasonable, relevant, and serve a purpose. With realistic goals, you can answer yes to the following questions:

- Is working toward this goal worthwhile?
- Is this the right time to set this goal?
- Does this goal match my efforts, desires, and needs?

T = *Time-Sensitive.* Time-sensitive goals are finite—they have a time frame or deadline. With time-sensitive goals, you can answer this question:

- When do I expect to tackle and attain this goal?

Below, Sari has transformed her earlier goal of increasing connection with her family by spending more quality time with her kids and husband into a values-based SMART goal. Use the spaces below each step to write your own responses for your own goal. You may want to check in with your psychotherapist for feedback after completing this activity.

How can I make this goal…

Specific?

Sari: *I want to spend time with my husband and kids because they are the most important relationships I have in my life. I will spend time with them on weeknights and weekends.*

You: _____

_____

_____

Measurable?

Sari: *I want to spend one hour three nights per week with my kids doing something they enjoy. I also want to spend one hour three times per week with my husband without the kids present. On the weekends, I want to spend five hours doing something as a family that we all enjoy.*

You: _____

_____

_____

Attainable and Adaptive?

Sari: *This goal is adaptive because it is directly in line with my values. It may not be attainable, because it conflicts with my schedule for intensive outpatient treatment in the evenings. Therefore, I'm going to revise my goal. During the week, I want to spend one hour two nights per week with my kids doing something they enjoy. I also want to spend one hour two times per week with my husband without the kids present. On the weekends, I want to spend five hours doing something as a family that we all enjoy.*

You: _____

_____

_____

Realistic?

Sari: *This goal is realistic and reasonable, as it will fit into my schedule for treatment and will improve my home environment, which will ultimately help me in my recovery.*

You: _____

_____

_____

Time-sensitive?

Sari: *I would like to have this schedule of two one-hour nights per week with my kids, two one-hour nights per week with my husband, and five hours on the weekends with my family put in place within the next month.*

You: _____

_____

_____

What is my final SMART goal?

Sari: *Within a one-month time frame, I will incorporate two one-hour nights with my children and two one-hour nights alone with my husband during the week when we will spend time doing something that my kids or my husband and I enjoy. I will also spend five hours with my family on the weekend doing something we all enjoy.*

You: _____

_____

_____

Breaking It Down and Getting Started

Now that we have established *why* you are choosing to continue through recovery (your values) and *how* you can go about putting these changes into place in your life (setting SMART goals), it is time to discuss *what* you need to do to persevere through this tough process. Related to values and goals, another core component of ACT is *committed action*, or taking deliberate and effective action that is guided and motivated by your values (Harris 2008). Committed action means doing whatever is effective for your recovery and persisting in hard times in order to live by your values. It also means recommitting to your values and refocusing on your goals after a lapse in your behavior; it means not throwing in the towel because of a slipup. It is through committed action that you persevere and continue to make progress in your recovery with your values as guidance and your goals as stepping stones for continuous growth.

Goals in recovery can feel overwhelming, and that can weaken your motivation to keep working on them. Attaining a goal is most effectively done by breaking it down into small, achievable steps. In ACT, you are often encouraged to ask yourself, *What is the tiniest, easiest, simplest step I can take to make progress toward my values and goals?* But how do you figure out the next tiny step to take?

To begin, you will need to create a timeline. This is an easy step when using SMART goals, because the *T* in SMART requires you to specify a time frame to complete your goal. Once you know how much time you are giving yourself, you can begin to fill in your timeline with smaller steps. When brainstorming smaller steps, try to break down each step into the smallest thing you can do. For example, if your goal is to spend more time in nature, you may choose hiking as a way to bring you closer to that goal. In order to go hiking, you may need to take the smaller steps of buying appropriate shoes, getting permission from your treatment team, and calling a friend to join you. If these steps still feel burdensome or are things you cannot do immediately, break them down even further. For example, you may need to save money to buy the shoes by putting aside $20 each week. Try to break your goal down into the smallest steps possible. Put them in chronological order and determine a realistic time frame for each step. Your time frame can range from within the next year to within the next day, depending on your main goal.

Let's put this process into action by completing the following activity. Sari has completed the exercise for you to use as a guide.

What is my main goal?

Sari: *Within a one-month time frame, I will incorporate two one-hour nights with my children and two one-hour nights alone with my husband during the week during which we will spend time doing something that my kids or my husband and I enjoy. I will also spend five hours with my family on the weekend doing something together that we all enjoy.*

Step 1: Create at timeline.

As I specified in my SMART goal, my timeline is *one month*.

Step 2: Identify all of the smaller steps that need to occur in order to progress toward your goal. Break down your steps as far as you can.

I need all of the following smaller goals to be attained in order to reach this goal:

- *Make a list of potential activities*
- *Collaborate with my husband regarding nights when he has the least amount of work*
- *Create a calendar to put on the refrigerator for the family to reference*
- *Buy any supplies necessary to participate in the activities on the list I create*
- *Figure out how much money we need to budget for any activities on the list that are not free*
- *Talk with my husband about my plan*
- *Talk with my kids about my plan*
- *Determine how I will deal with needing to be flexible when the schedule needs to change*
- *Buy a planner for myself to help keep all of my appointments, quality time, and other responsibilities in order*

- *Put plan into action and have a week during which I fulfill each part of my goal*

- *Evaluate its effectiveness and make changes accordingly*

Step 3: Put your list of steps in chronological order, from the first step to the last.

1. *Talk with my husband about my plan*

2. *Talk with my kids about my plan*

3. *Collaborate with my husband regarding nights when he has the least amount of work*

4. *Buy a planner for myself to help keep all of my appointments, quality time, and other responsibilities in order*

5. *Make a list of potential activities*

6. *Figure out how much money we need to budget for any activities on the list that are not free*

7. *Buy any supplies necessary to participate in the activities on the list I create*

8. *Create a calendar to put on the refrigerator for the family to reference*

9. *Determine how I will deal with needing to be flexible when the schedule needs to change*

10. *Put plan into action and have a week during which I fulfill each part of my goal*

11. *Evaluate its effectiveness and make changes accordingly*

Step 4: Fill in your timeline using your identified steps. Use the parentheses to specify the appropriate smaller time frames for your steps (e.g., one year, six months, one week).

- What can I realistically accomplish (*in the next four weeks*) that will get me closer to my goal? *Determine how I will deal with needing to be flexible when the schedule needs to change. Put plan into action and have a week during which I fulfill each part of my goal. Evaluate its effectiveness and make changes accordingly.*

- What can I realistically accomplish (*in the next three weeks*) that will get me closer to my goal? *Buy any supplies necessary to participate in the activities on the list I create. Create a calendar to put on the refrigerator for the family to reference.*

- What can I realistically accomplish (*in the next two weeks*) that will get me closer to my goal? *Figure out how much money we need to budget for any activities on the list that are not free. Buy any supplies necessary to participate in the activities on the list I create.*

- What can I realistically accomplish (*in the next week*) that will get me closer to my goal? *Buy a planner for myself to help keep all of my appointments, quality time, and other responsibilities in order. Make a list of potential activities.*

- What can I realistically accomplish (*in the next day*) that will get me closer to my goal? *Talk with my kids about my plan. Collaborate with my husband regarding nights when he has the least amount of work.*

- What can I realistically accomplish (*in this moment*) that will get me closer to my goal? *Talk with my husband about my plan.*

Now it's your turn—take some time to outline the smaller goals you can make and the steps you can to take to ultimately reach your goal. This exercise is also available at http://www.newharbinger.com/39348.

What is my main goal? _____

_____

_____

Step 1: Create at timeline.

As I specified in my SMART outline, my timeline is _____.

Step 2: Identify all of the smaller steps that need to occur in order to progress toward your goal. Break down your steps as far as you can.

I need all of the following smaller goals to be attained in order to reach this goal:

- _____
- _____
- _____
- _____
- _____
- _____
- _____
- _____
- _____
- _____

Step 3: Put your list of steps in chronological order, from the first step to the last.

1. _____

2. _____

3. _____

4. _____

5. _____

6. _____

7. _____

8. _____

9. _____

10. _____

Step 4: Fill in your timeline using your identified steps. Use the parentheses to specify the appropriate smaller time frames for your steps (e.g., one year, six months, one week).

- What can I realistically accomplish in (_____) that will get me closer to my goal?

_____

_____

- What can I realistically accomplish in (_____) that will get me closer to my goal?

_____

_____

- What can I realistically accomplish in (_____) that will get me closer to my goal?

_____

_____

- What can I realistically accomplish in (_____) that will get me closer to my goal?

_____

_____

Maintaining Motivation to Reach Your Goals

Understanding your values and setting goals for yourself is the easy part. The hard part is continually committing to your recovery multiple times a day. It is difficult to maintain motivation every single day, especially during periods of stress and distress. However, it is important that you find something to motivate you, even if it is something external (such as a job or another person's well-being) rather than internal (like wanting recovery because you want it and feel you deserve it). Sometimes we need external motivators until we can foster internal motivation or in times when our internal motivation fades. Maintaining motivation is extremely important throughout the recovery process, and it will be discussed in detail in the next chapter. Before moving on, check out Sari's motivators, and then take some time to write your ideas in the space on the opposite page. Keep these motivators in mind as you move on to chapter 7.

External Motivators	Internal Motivators
My job	My values
My relationship with my husband	Wanting to be a good mother
My children's well-being	Wanting to be a good partner
Staying out of inpatient treatment	Wanting to feel a sense of inner peace
Not disappointing my treatment team	I want to lead a meaningful life
Not disappointing my family	I want to give back to others

What are *your* external and internal sources of motivation?

External Motivators	Internal Motivators

Journaling Pages

In this chapter, we discussed the process and importance of identifying your core values and how to use them to create goals. We also talked about creating SMART goals; how to break down your goals into small, manageable steps; and motivators for pursuing recovery-based goals. What reactions or experiences did you have as you completed the exercises in this chapter? Maybe it felt difficult to narrow down your core values, or perhaps you felt too overwhelmed by your goals and you struggled to narrow them down into smaller steps. What barriers do you anticipate coming up for you as you move forward with your recovery-oriented goals? Both internal barriers (like anxiety, negative self-talk, memories of past trauma) and external barriers (like lack of resources, others' judgments, conflict with friends or family) can come up as you work toward your goals. Use the space below to reflect on both your experiences in these activities and the barriers you anticipate coming up for you as you move forward in recovery. Consider sharing these thoughts and ideas with your treatment team members.

_____

_____

_____

_____

_____

_____

_____

_____

_____

_____

_____

Chapter 7

Maintaining Motivation Through Recovery

Motivation is the fuel, necessary to keep the human engine running.

—Zig Ziglar

Meet Max

Max has been actively working on his recovery for nearly a year. Throughout the year, he has alternated between periods of strong motivation and progress in his recovery and lapses in which he has reengaged in restricting, overexercising, and losing weight. When his motivation is high, and when he keeps focus on his values (his connections to friends and family and being a responsible person) and the steps he needs to take to achieve his long-term goals (working in the medical field), he does well. But Max puts significant pressure on himself to maintain his progress—he greatly fears becoming the kind of irresponsible and ineffectual person his father was—so any slip or urge to engage in eating disordered behaviors feels like a failure and quickly extinguishes his motivation. At that point, he berates himself up and gives in to his eating disorder, feeling that he will never recover. Max has found several ways to pull himself out of this kind of lapse, especially by picking apart the negative self-talk in his mind and recognizing how illogical it is ("Why did I just think that I'm doomed to fail this class? Most of my grades have been excellent!"). He also uses mindfulness practices to quiet his mind. Nevertheless, this vacillation in his progress has left him frustrated with himself; recovery often just feels too overwhelming and burdensome. He recognizes that perceiving recovery as unmanageable causes him to lose motivation to keep progressing, which contributes to his lapses into eating disordered behaviors and creates a greater sense of hopelessness. He feels stuck in this cycle, as he struggles to find reasons to continue moving forward in recovery.

Why Recovery from Anorexia Can Be So Hard

In chapter 6, we discussed how understanding your values and setting goals for yourself is just the beginning in making changes—and is often the "easy" part. As Max's story demonstrates, the hard part is maintaining the motivation hour after hour and day after day, keeping a focus on the motivations behind your actions, taking necessary and effective steps toward recovery, and making healthy and adaptive choices that will move you in the direction of your values and goals. Cultivating and maintaining motivation is particularly difficult for individuals with anorexia. Unlike many other mental illnesses, anorexia tends to be *ego-syntonic*, which means that individuals with anorexia experience their symptoms, behaviors, and thoughts as being consistent with their self-image and desires (Guarda 2008). Restricting, exercising, and losing weight, for example, are rewarding in some way (they help you cope, they give you a sense of accomplishment or self-worth, or they feel good). That is not to say people with anorexia never hate having an eating disorder; most would agree that the repercussions of having an eating disorder are not consistent with their desires or values—repercussions that include the negative physical side effects (bone loss, bloating and constipation, hair loss, brittle nails, heart problems, dizziness or passing out, fatigue, difficulty sleeping, damage to teeth) and other side effects (poor relationships, inability to focus, self-hatred, withdrawal and isolation, and risk of death). However, the ego-syntonic aspects of anorexia do exist, making it especially difficult to make the choices that will guide you further in recovery every day, regardless of triggering situations or intense emotions.

Extrinsic Motivation Versus Intrinsic Motivation

There are two types of motivation that influence how we behave: extrinsic motivation and intrinsic motivation. Extrinsic motivation comes from external sources outside of yourself (like attending psychotherapy appointments to avoid late-fee charges), while intrinsic motivation comes from internal resources within yourself (attending psychotherapy appointments because you want to get better). Because anorexia tends to be ego-syntonic, fostering intrinsic motivation is often extremely difficult. Hence, it is typically easier to be successful in recovery in intensive treatment settings than in outpatient settings or with no treatment. Intensive treatment settings establish various types of external motivators that help you take positive steps toward recovery (for example, gaining privileges if you complete meals, or adding nutritional supplements to your meal plan if you do not complete meals). However, once you step down to less structured levels of treatment, the amount of extrinsic motivation tends to decrease and the consequences and rewards of your behaviors are not as immediate.

Having both external and internal motivators is important in recovery and in life. The more sources of motivation you have, the more likely you are to continue in a healthy, recovery-oriented direction. Because intrinsic motivation is not always stable—as there will inevitably be days when you want to give up—it is important to create and identify external sources of motivation for yourself. However, relying solely on external motivators can be detrimental to your recovery in the long term, as the value you place on them is likely to dissipate gradually over time. Intrinsic motivation is long lasting and will foster a stronger and more stable recovery journey. Therefore, rather than relying on extrinsic motivation as a crutch, use it to help foster intrinsic motivation. Sometimes you will need to go through the motions in recovery (for example, by following your treatment team's recommendations regardless of your feelings toward its members). At those times, external motivators (such as not wanting to disappoint others, avoiding a higher level of care, or getting or remaining medically stable) will serve you well. They will help you to avoid a lapse or relapse and prevent you from falling so far backward physically that your mental health and well-being are compromised. But eventually you will need to make choices that move you toward recovery for *you*, because *you* want it and because *you* are ready to live in accordance with your values. Having intrinsic motivation does not mean you are ready or able to do recovery alone; it means quite the opposite: that you are ready to do whatever it takes, including using the help offered to you and the level of support that will best assist you at this time, to make steps toward recovery without the need of external rewards or consequences to motivate you. Some examples of intrinsic motivators for recovery include your values that you identified in the previous chapter, a desire to live a more vital life than you live when you are engaged in your eating disorder, and goals you have for yourself that may be possible to achieve only with recovery (such as to finish school, pursue your dream job, have a stable relationship, go on an adventure)

Now that we have discussed the differences between and importance of both extrinsic and intrinsic motivation, take some time to write yourself a letter on *your* motivation and reasons to recover. Why do you want recovery? What keeps you motivated to recover? Be sure to include a list of both your external and internal motivators, including those items you identified as motivators at the end of chapter 6. This list may need to be reviewed time to time both as a reminder and in order to keep it updated and relevant to you. While you can complete this exercise at any time in your recovery, it would be best to write your letter when you are feeling particularly motivated. Keep this letter handy and read it when you are struggling with motivation or having urges to act on eating disordered behaviors. Feel free to add to it or rewrite it at any time, as your life may change and provide you with more or different reasons to stay motivated. Take a look at Max's letter for some inspiration before writing your own.

Dear Max,

If you are reading this, you likely need a pep talk and some reminders for why you should continue fighting for recovery. First and foremost, you need to be healthy in order to finish your degree and to be successful in your career. You have wanted to be a pediatric nurse for so long, and you have worked too hard to let your eating disorder take this away from you. Also, think about the connections you have made so far in recovery. Remember how awful you felt when you were so isolated before recovery. Don't let yourself get back to that. You need to keep working on your recovery so you can maintain those friendships. You also need to continue in your recovery because weight restoration sucks! If you lose the weight, you will just need to put it back on at some point, and you know how horrible that process feels, both physically and mentally. I know in the past your recovery journey was unstable, and you lost hope easily when urges or slips occurred. Don't let a slip turn into a relapse! You can make the next healthy decision rather than giving up because you "already messed up." You have recommitted to recovery before, and you can do it again. So keep on fighting hard, even through tough days like today!

—Max

Now write your letter. It may be useful to share this letter with your psychotherapist in order to process your thoughts and expand upon your lists of reasons to recover.

_____

_____

_____

_____

_____

_____

_____

_____

_____

_____

_____

_____

Setting Yourself Up for Success

In addition to identifying and utilizing your external and internal sources of motivation, there are ways you can reinforce your hard work in your recovery. Just as setting goals is not sufficient for action, sometimes motivation is also not enough. Motivation waxes and wanes for everyone. Rather than try to avoid the dips in feeling motivated for recovery, accept them as natural and let yourself experience them, but not before you set up a safety net and supports that can help you get back up and be ready to fight. Try the following ideas from dialectical behavior therapy (Linehan 1993), cognitive behavioral therapy (Beck 2011), and acceptance and commitment therapy (Hayes, Strosahl, and Wilson 2012) to help you set yourself up for success. Use them even when you are highly motivated for recovery, so when you are feeling more apathetic, taking these steps will not seem foreign or uncomfortable. You are more likely to continue the following behaviors if you integrate them into your daily life, as opposed to starting using them when you are feeling less motivated—because why would you want to start something new if your problem is that you are not motivated in the first place?

Create Accountability

Create accountability by telling your friends or family about your goals and what you are working on in your recovery. By committing to someone else that you will take specific steps or actions, you create a sense of purpose (*I can't go for a run, because I promised my friend I would refrain, and I do not want to lie or break my promise.*). Another way to create accountability is setting up contracts with your treatment team members. For example, your team can create a contract that states specific intentions and actions you will and will not take for a certain period of time. This physical documentation of your commitment to certain goals is sometimes sufficient for an extra boost of motivation. Also, knowing someone will be checking in with you periodically to follow up on how you are progressing toward the agreed-upon goals can motivate you to stay on track. For some people, outlining consequences for if the contract is not upheld may also be useful.

Take Responsibility

In addition to creating accountability, it is important to take responsibility for your actions. Thus, if you do catch yourself doing something that is detracting from your recovery, it is important that you set up a system with your treatment team, your family, or your friends where you come clean about any behaviors, attitudes, or thinking patterns that are not helping your recovery or are not in line with your values and goals. You may also want to set a goal for how you plan to address the issue and share that with others as well.

Try completing the following exercise to begin thinking of ways to create accountability for yourself and to take responsibility when you notice yourself engaging in eating disordered behaviors or thought patterns. Try to answer each of the following questions for a variety of behaviors or thinking patterns that you are most susceptible to and that will most likely affect your recovery. Max's responses are provided as guidance. This exercise is also available at http://www.newharbinger.com/39348.

What do I need to be held accountable for?	Who can hold me accountable for this?	How will I take responsibility?	Will there be consequences if I engage in this behavior?	What goal can I set for myself to refocus on my recovery?
Exercising	My boyfriend	I will tell him each time I go to the gym and how much time I spent there.	If I spend more than thirty minutes at the gym three or more times, he can tell my team in case I haven't.	I will call my boyfriend when I have the urge to exercise and wait one hour before making the decision to go.

Celebrate Small Successes

Focusing solely on ways in which you fall short is never helpful. It is important to share your successes with others, no matter how small they seem. In recovery, no success or step toward recovery is insignificant or unworthy of praise; they all are important and, taken together, add up to you making progress and achieving your recovery goals. Share and celebrate successes along the way. Reward yourself in a healthy way for taking steps toward recovery. You do not have to wait until you achieve a lofty or long-term goal to be proud of yourself. And the steps you make toward recovery don't have to be perfect; a step away from recovery does not negate or take away from your positive, adaptive, and healthy step. Avoid statements such as *I followed through with spending time with my friends tonight instead of isolating, but I wasn't talkative and was in my head the whole time. There isn't much to celebrate.* Instead, remember that spending time with friends was a small but significant step in the right direction, and the quality of the interaction does not take away from the fact that you stepped out of your comfort zone and chose to be social when isolation seemed easier. You can use the second part of that statement ("I wasn't talkative and was in my head the whole time.") to take some accountability, as described above, for not being present. Then, set the goal of being more present and mindful of your attention the next time you are with friends.

What are some small successes you have made in recovery so far that you can take the time to celebrate? Just as Max did below, write down your successes and ideas for celebrating. Remember that celebrations do not have to be huge parties that you throw yourself each time you progress in recovery. The simple act of sharing your success with a friend who will be proud of or happy for you is a way to celebrate.

Small Success: *I ate ice cream for dessert when I went out for dinner.*

Ways to Celebrate: *Share this with my treatment team and boyfriend; take time tomorrow to relax and watch a movie; congratulate myself and be excited for myself.*

Small Success: _____

Ways to Celebrate: _____

_____

Small Success: _____

Ways to Celebrate: _____

_____

Small Success: _____

Ways to Celebrate: _____

_____

Be Mindful

Mindfulness is the practice of being aware and staying present. It is taking time to observe, describe, and engage in things that are happening right now. Much of our time is spent thinking about the past or future rather than the present moment. This is not always a negative thing, as we need to think about the past to learn from our experiences and about the future to set goals for ourselves and give us direction in life. However, spending too much attention on the past and future can cause depression or anxiety and is not helpful for moving forward to achieve our goals. When you are caught up in your eating disordered thoughts or behaviors, it is hard to be present in other areas of your life. It makes connecting with others, pursuing goals, and working toward your values difficult. Being mindful means being in the present moment, paying attention to what is happening in the here and now. Be mindful of your intentions behind your behaviors. Be mindful of your thoughts; notice your thoughts. Be present in your day-to-day affairs rather than dwelling on things in the past or worrying about something that may happen in the future. By being mindful, you can take a step back and observe your mind (your thoughts, urges, emotions, and memories) without immediately acting on these internal experiences. You can create some space between these experiences and your behaviors. The more space you can develop between what goes on in your mind and how you act, the more control you can feel over your eating disorder. But remember that mindfulness takes practice. Be patient with yourself as you practice these skills.

To help develop a stronger practice of mindfulness, you can start by taking time each day to notice your breath, the way your body reacts to air being pumped in and out of your body, and your thoughts as you attend to your breathing. Try it for two minutes at first and work your way up to ten minutes. Like Max has done, jot down reactions and what you notice as you complete this exercise each time you practice.

Max: Practice #1

How long did I practice? *Two minutes*

What did I notice? *I noticed how cold the air was as it entered my nose and that it was warm as it exited my mouth. I noticed my feet on the floor and the weight of my body on the chair. I noticed my mind wandering a lot, and I found myself judging my body and feeling uncomfortable in my body. I noticed that I had to bring my attention back to my breath many times. I noticed my heart beating, my chest and stomach rising and falling, and the sound of the fan moving.*

Practice #1

How long did I practice? _____

What did I notice? _____

_____

_____

_____

Practice #2

How long did I practice? _____

What did I notice? _____

_____

_____

_____

Practice #3

How long did I practice? _____

What did I notice? _____

_____

_____

_____

Other mindfulness practices include paying attention to your senses one at a time. For example, close your eyes and identify ten things you hear. This may be difficult at first, but follow through with the exercise until you reach ten sounds. Next, focus on touch or physical sensations. Without moving from where you are sitting, identify ten things you can feel (for example, your heart beating or the texture of your pants) and describe the sensations with one word. Finally, focus your attention on a single object. Name ten things you observe in that object using your sense of sight. Try to stick to facts about the object (e.g., the flower has six petals) rather than judgments (the flower is pretty). Take some time to practice with each of these senses and reflect on what you notice each time in the space below.

Practice #1 (Hearing)

What did I notice? _____

_____

_____

_____

Practice #2 (Touch)

What did I notice? _____

_____

_____

_____

Practice #3 (Sight)

What did I notice? _____

_____

_____

_____

Make Use of Your Support System

We discussed above the idea of involving others to help you take accountability. It is important to utilize your support system as much as possible, as members of your support system can remind you why you are working toward recovery, and they can help you to succeed. Reaching out to others for support and actively using them for support in recovery is not a sign of weakness, but one of strength, in that you are more fully using all available resources in your life to be successful in recovery. Establishing and utilizing your support system will be discussed in more detail in chapter 10; for now, let's think about how you can use members of your support system specifically with regard to meeting your goals and maintaining the motivation to do so. Think of ways specific friends or family members can actively help you achieve certain goals, keeping the following in mind:

- The people you put in your support system must want you to succeed and become healthy.

- The people in your support system may not know what to do to help. We often get mad when others do not meet our needs or understand what we need from them; however, this frustration is often a result of not directly communicating specifically how we want or need others to act. Thus, it is important to be specific when explaining to your friends, family members, or treatment team members what it is you need from them.

- Everyone has strengths and weaknesses, including each member of your support system. Think about what specific things you would find helpful in meeting your goals and maintaining motivation. Pick specific people to ask for their support and assistance based on their strengths.

Take some time to complete the following exercise to identify who currently fulfills each role and who could also potentially fulfill that role. Add any other important roles your supporters can fulfill to help you in your recovery.

Role	Who currently fulfills this role?	Who else could fulfill this role?
Feedback *Those whom you can count on to give you honest feedback in ways that you can hear.*		
Self-Disclosure *Those with whom you can be truly authentic and honest.*		
Balance *Those in your life who help you with maintaining balance in your life. This can be someone who reminds you to take a break or who is there to engage in self-care activities.*		
Validation *Those whom you can count on to validate your experiences, thoughts, and emotions. This does not necessarily mean they agree with you, but they are able to understand and support you.*		
Fun *Those in your life with whom you have fun.*		
(insert role)		

Common Pitfalls

Staying motivated in recovery requires a significant amount of self-awareness and honesty. Staying 100 percent motivated all the time is an unreasonable and unrealistic expectation. Recovery is not always pleasant. It is hard work and is often more of an "Ugh…recovery" experience—not "Yay, recovery!" There are plenty of times when apathy takes over, and you struggle to make even the tiniest step toward your values and goals. It is important to expect those moments and allow yourself to experience your emotions that are related to your low level of motivation. It is equally as important to pick yourself back up to get back on track before a pattern of slipups spirals into a relapse. Thus, acknowledging times when you will be prone to making choices that move you away from your values and goals and identifying the signs that you are slipping is important. If you do not notice you are slipping, you cannot change your behaviors or know that it is time to reach out for help. These pitfalls—times that make you vulnerable to decreased motivation—are common in the recovery process. Below are some typical pitfalls in maintaining motivation through recovery. Take some time to identify which of these are relevant to you, and add your own potential pitfalls in the space at the end.

Emotional Arousal

When experiencing too much anxiety and stress, you may develop a sense of hopelessness and feel overwhelmed, which will inevitably decrease your ability to think rationally, concentrate, and focus. Without such cognitive processes in place, your anxiety and stress essentially paralyze you, and you create a self-fulfilling prophecy. For example, you may end up creating situations in which you are unable to succeed because of the intense levels of anticipatory anxiety about not being able to succeed.

Suggested Solution—Take time for self-care or to engage in relaxation and mindfulness exercises (see chapters 11 and 12). Taking time to participate in activities that you enjoy helps your ability to feel productive, clear minded, levelheaded, efficacious, and satisfied with yourself. Relaxation and mindfulness exercises help you to be aware of your emotions, remain present, let go of fears and worries, and decrease anxiety. You may add to this list once you complete chapters 11 and 12, but take a moment right now to list three ways you can help yourself relax when you are feeling intense emotions.

_____

_____

_____

Avoidance of Discomfort

A common pitfall you may find yourself falling into is only creating goals or taking steps that are comfortable. You are likely highly motivated most of the time to take comfortable steps toward your values-based goals and recovery, but your motivation to truly challenge yourself could be lacking. Of course, comfortable steps are necessary and useful, but by avoiding any sense of discomfort, you are avoiding a significant portion of your recovery. For example, if you are meeting your meal plan but sticking rigidly to specific foods because you are fearful of increasing the variety of foods you eat, you are doing enough to maintain your weight, but you are still living by a set of eating disordered rules. Recovery is not typically a comfortable process, so if you find yourself complacent and consistently comfortable, you may want to take a step back and evaluate what steps in your recovery you are avoiding.

Suggested Solution—Take hold of your committed action and do what is uncomfortable. If it scares you, it is likely a worthwhile feat to overcome. Create an honest list of behaviors or experiences you are avoiding but would be beneficial to your recovery. Answer the following questions to help you begin creating this list. Share this list with the people in your support system, particularly your treatment team, and make a conscious effort to tackle one or two challenges each week, keeping in mind that many challenges may need to be integrated into your recovery long term.

What events (e.g., parties, going out to eat) do you avoid? What about them is uncomfortable for you?

_____

_____

_____

What foods (i.e., fear foods) do you avoid?

_____

_____

_____

What kinds of emotional expression (e.g., being vulnerable and authentic with others, keeping your feelings to yourself) are most uncomfortable for you? Which ones do you tend to avoid?

_____

_____

_____

What are some unhealthy behaviors (e.g., not weighing yourself, not counting calories) you are avoiding giving up? What is keeping you from letting go of them?

_____

_____

_____

What types of interpersonal interactions (e.g., using direct communication or lying by omission regarding your behaviors, thoughts, and progress) do you avoid?

_____

_____

_____

Denial

Because anorexia is ego-syntonic, denial is common. Being in denial—lacking the self-awareness to recognize the reality of your situation, behaviors, or thoughts—is a dangerous barrier to your recovery. The inability to be objective and introspective that characterizes denial makes it dangerous, because insight is necessary for self-initiated change. For example, you may be in denial that your exercise regimen is compulsive; you may truly believe and insist that you are choosing to exercise for the "right" reasons; and you may deny feeling compelled to exercise to feel balanced, to reduce anxiety, or to burn calories.

Suggested Solution—Denial and defensiveness often go hand in hand. If you or others around you are noticing that you are becoming defensive, irritable, or short tempered when others challenge your behaviors or thoughts, you should take that as a sign that you may be in denial. If you were not in denial, you would likely be able to react more calmly and rationally and take others' concerns into consideration. Because of the lack of self-awareness you experience in denial, it is important to plan for times of denial while you are in a healthy state of mind. Identify ways you are likely to react or ways you have acted in the past when you were in denial about something related to your eating disorder. Collaborate with others, particularly your treatment team, and determine the most effective way others can approach you if they believe you are in denial. Commit to yourself and to members of your support system that you will do your best to take a step back and think about their concerns objectively. What ways may indicate that you are in denial? How can others approach you about their concerns? Follow Max's example in the space below.

Signs I'm in Denial: *I may get defensive and irritable; I may avoid the topic.*

How Others Can Respond: *Expressing their feelings and concern instead of accusing me of being in denial; be firm in telling me the reality of the situation, even when I don't want to hear it.*

Signs I'm in Denial: _____

_____

How Others Can Respond: _____

_____

_____

_____

Feeling Stuck

There are going to be many times when you feel stuck in your recovery, which will likely make you feel worn down and defeated. You may feel like you are just going through the motions and that you simply cannot fight this hard every day for the rest of your life. You may recognize the progress you have made but feel like the amount of effort it will take to reach your next set of recovery goals is too much. You are tired of fighting; you do not want to go back to your eating disorder, but you do not want to keep fighting.

Suggested Solution—Call upon your external sources of motivation. Feeling stuck is the ultimate level of apathy; it is when you are going to experience the lowest level of internal motivation. It is during this type of pitfall when you should engage as much as possible with your external sources of motivation, rather than reading a list of internal reasons to continue fighting. Connect with friends, call your family, or reach out to your treatment team. Pick one of your values and do something that brings you closer to it (take a walk through nature, read a book, paint, do yoga, call a friend, go to church, visit an animal shelter, or plan a get-together with your peers or coworkers). Take time to practice self-care, engaging in an activity that you truly enjoy. What are three things you can *do* when you are feeling stuck in recovery?

Forgetting the "Whys"

It is important to remember *why* you are fighting for recovery. It is a long and effortful journey, and it is common to fall into the trap of going through the motions mindlessly or wanting to give up because it does not feel worth it. In either case, you have likely forgotten *why* you are striving for your goals and for a long-lasting recovery. Max, for example, often finds himself stuck in a cycle of frustration with himself and recovery when things do not go smoothly. When this happens, his focus and attention shift from why recovery is important for him to his negative judgments of himself and his struggles. It can be easy to get caught up in feeling hopeless, frustrated, ineffective, or overwhelmed in recovery.

Suggested Solution—Create a list for yourself noting all that you will maintain or gain through recovery (e.g., connection with others, a career, stable health and well-being, peace of mind, or pleasurable emotions) and all that you stand to lose through relapse (your health, relationships, time wasted engaging in eating disorder behaviors, your education, or a meaningful life). Also, the values that you identified in chapter 6 are your core reasons for recovery. Add these to your list. Read this list, add to it, and involve others in helping you remember the reasons you are working so hard in recovery. Begin your list in the space below. To help you generate your list, ask yourself questions like: What *am I living for? What will I give up if I relapse? What are the benefits of being in recovery? Why did I choose recovery in the first place?* and *What have I gained in my life since starting recovery?*

Cognitive Distortions

Your thoughts can do some unhealthy and maladaptive things as you progress through recovery. There are a variety of identified cognitive distortions that negatively influence our emotions and behaviors, according to cognitive behavioral therapy (CBT), an evidence-based and commonly used approach in treating eating disorders (Galsworthy-Francis and Allan 2014). Similar to distortions, be wary of "should" statements (e.g., "I *should* be recovered by now" or "I *shouldn't* have to eat this much each day"). All of these indicate some fallacy in your thinking. The following list of cognitive distortions includes examples from Max illustrating how some of his cognitive distortions and "should" statements play a part in his recovery. Try to add an example of your own under each of his.

All-or-Nothing Thinking (Dichotomous Thinking)—Viewing something as all good or all bad, with no gradation in between.

Max's example: *Either I complete my full meal plan, or I'm failing at recovery.*

_____

_____

Selective Abstraction—Picking out an idea or fact from an event to support your negative thinking.

Max's example: *I wasn't invited to their study group. See—everyone thinks I'm annoying. (Meanwhile, Max was invited to join another study group with his friends from class.)*

_____

_____

Mind reading—Believing that you know what another person is thinking about you.

Max's example: *Everyone at dinner is thinking how disgusting I am for eating all of this food.*

_____

_____

Negative prediction—Belief that something bad is going to happen when there is no evidence to support it.

Max's example: *I just know that if I gain weight, I won't be able to stop. (Meanwhile, Max has never been overweight and has never struggled with overeating or bingeing.)*

_____

_____

Catastrophizing—Taking one event you are concerned about and exaggerating it so that you become fearful.

Max's example: *Recovery is too hard; I'm never going to recover.*

_____

_____

Overgeneralization—Making a rule based on a limited number of negative events.

Max's example: *I said something awkward twice now while out with friends. I'm such an annoying and awkward person!*

_____

_____

Labeling and mislabeling—Viewing yourself negatively based on some errors or mistakes.

Max's example: *My dietitian said my weight has dropped a little since our last appointment. I'm such a failure.*

_____

_____

Magnification or minimization—Magnifying imperfections or minimizing good points that lead to conclusions that support belief of inferiority and a feeling of depression.

Max's example: *I got a C on my biology exam. I'm never going to become a nurse. (Meanwhile, Max got As on his previous two exams.)*

_____

_____

Personalization—Taking an event that is unrelated to you and making it meaningful.

Max's example: *Johnny was talking before class with a small group that I wasn't part of; clearly it's because I'm annoying.*

_____

_____

Suggested Solution—In CBT, it is important to identify maladaptive thinking patterns, such as cognitive distortions, and actively challenge or reframe them. There are many ways you can challenge or reframe your maladaptive thoughts: identify evidence for and against your thought or belief and determine which side has the most quality evidence; evaluate the probability that your thought or belief is true and accurate; brainstorm all possible alternatives to explaining the situation; or play devil's advocate with yourself by arguing against your identified distortion. You may wish to use a daily thought record and work with your psychotherapist to process and discuss difficulties related to your cognitions. With a daily thought record, we can add to the exercise you just completed. You can (1) write down maladaptive thoughts you catch yourself having throughout the day and label the type of distortion, just as we did in the previous exercise, then (2) name the emotions that are elicited from that thought and rate them on a scale of 1 to 10 (with higher numbers meaning greater intensity of that emotion); (3) challenge the thought, using one of the above techniques; (4) write down an alternative, more adaptive way of thinking about the situation; and (5) reevaluate how intense you are feeling the emotions you originally listed. Max completed his daily thought record as an example below.

Maladaptive Thought: *Recovery is too hard. I'm never going to recover. Why try?*

Type of Distortion: *Negative prediction and all-or-nothing thinking.*

Emotions and Ratings	Challenge	Adaptive Thought	Emotions and Ratings
Hopeless (10) Sad (8) Angry (6)	*I have gained weight, made friends, and expanded my food choices. I have made progress.*	*Recovery is hard, but it is also possible. I've definitely made progress so far. I can only recover if I try.*	Hopeless (6) Sad (3) Angry (4)

Using Max's examples as a guide, try to complete your own. This daily thought record is available at http://www.newharbinger.com/39348, so you can complete it more than once. It can be helpful to fill it out each day to help you track your thoughts and your progress in identifying, challenging, and reacting to them.

Maladaptive Thought: _____

Type of Distortion: _____

Emotions and Ratings	Challenge	Adaptive Thought	Emotions and Ratings

Maladaptive Thought: _____

Type of Distortion: _____

Emotions and Ratings	Challenge	Adaptive Thought	Emotions and Ratings

Maladaptive Thought: _____

Type of Distortion: _____

Emotions and Ratings	Challenge	Adaptive Thought	Emotions and Ratings

Rationalization

Another way your thoughts may hinder your recovery is through rationalization—which basically means making excuses. If you are rationalizing, you are explaining why engaging in your eating disorder (behaviorally, cognitively, or emotionally) is logical, while avoiding the true reasons behind your actions and thoughts. Some other ways you may find yourself rationalizing include convincing yourself that you are recovered despite engaging in certain eating disordered behaviors or ways of thinking, insisting your eating disorder is "not that bad" and thus you do not need to follow through with treatment or your goals, and blaming others or your environment for you engaging in eating disordered behaviors.

Suggested Solution—Think about experiences or behaviors you have rationalized in the past. Collaborate with your friends, family, and treatment team members, as they may be able to give you more accurate and objective accounts of ways you tend to rationalize. Taking note of them while you are in a healthy frame of mind can give you tangible evidence to reflect back on when you are noticing you are slipping or lacking motivation. Determine what would be effective ways for others to react when they hear you making such statements, and ask them to respond as such. Like Max has done below, take some time to list a rationalization you recall making in the past and write down one way others can helpfully respond when they hear such statements from you in the future.

Max's Rationalization: *I only weigh myself once a day, so it's really not a big deal.*

How Others Can Respond: *Remind me that I get obsessed with my weight easily and express their concern for my behavior.*

My Rationalization: _____

How Others Can Respond: _____

_____

Facing Triggers

Triggers (i.e., people, images, situations, behaviors, emotions, thoughts, discussions, or comments that elicit or increase your urges to engage in eating disordered behaviors and thoughts) are inevitable. And when triggers are present, you may find yourself being motivated to resort to your eating disorder as opposed to recovery. As with Max, who is often triggered by small slips, negative self-talk, weighing himself, and exercising in a gym instead of outdoors, triggers can have a strong pull and can change the way you are thinking, behaving, or perceiving reality.

Suggested Solution—Depending on the specific trigger, there are several options for handling the situation:

- You can avoid some triggers, particularly if you are in a vulnerable state (that is, you can avoid social media outlets where people, images, or posts are likely to trigger you). What triggers can you avoid without sacrificing your values?

_____

_____

_____

- Triggers are not always avoidable (e.g., a family gatherings, commercials, or conflicts). In these cases, you can use coping skills that help you distract yourself from the triggers or tolerate your discomfort and emotional reactions to them (see chapter 12). What ways do you currently cope with unavoidable triggers?

_____

_____

_____

- You can also reframe the triggering situations. For example, you can remind yourself that although someone appears to be able to hold on to thinness while also being successful in other areas of life, you are not seeing the whole picture. Recall how horrible you likely felt when you were actively engaging in your eating disorder. These feelings are pervasive with eating disorders; one cannot live a meaningful life with an eating disorder. What is one way you can reframe a triggering situation that can help you stay focused on your recovery?

_____

_____

_____

- It is also important to remember that, as mentioned, triggers are unavoidable. Even if they are unavoidable, you have the power to separate or detach yourself from them. An image of a thin girl or someone jogging past your house is not inherently triggering. It acts as a trigger only because of your interpretation and the pattern of thoughts that occur in your mind as a result. Try to detach yourself from these thoughts. You can do this by either reframing them or accepting them and recognizing them for what they are—thoughts. A good mantra to keep in mind is "A thought is not an order, and my thoughts do not need to become actions." What mantra can you keep in mind to help you detach from triggers?

_____

_____

_____

- Work with your psychotherapist on developing insight as to why specific things are triggering for you. What is the meaning behind your triggers, and what is pulling you to act on your eating disorder when they are present? Begin to brainstorm and elicit the help of your psychotherapist to identify your triggers, determine the most effective ways for you to deal with them, and understand why such things invoke an increased desire to self-destruct or sabotage your recovery. Reflect on these points below and share your thoughts with your psychotherapist to help jump-start the conversation.

_____

_____

_____

Journaling Pages

In this chapter, we discussed extrinsic and intrinsic motivation, why motivation is difficult to maintain for individuals with anorexia, ways to increase your likelihood of succeeding, and potential struggles you might face in maintaining motivation. Before moving on to another chapter, take a moment to reflect on the work you completed in this chapter and write about your reactions in the space below. What emotions came up for you as you worked through this chapter? Perhaps there were times you felt frustrated, hopeful, hopeless, excited, or overwhelmed. Take some time to check in with yourself emotionally and consider sharing these reflections with your psychotherapist.

_____

_____

_____

_____

_____

_____

_____

_____

_____

_____

_____

_____

_____

_____

Chapter 8

Learning to Accept Your Self

What lies behind us and what lies before us are small matters compared to what lies within us.

—Oliver Wendell Holmes

Meet Chloe

After struggling with anorexia for four years, Chloe has finally decided to seek help. For the past six months, she has been working with an outpatient team. Most of her work thus far has been focused on weight restoration, improving her compliance with her meal plan, and exploring the relationship between how she feels about herself and her recovery. She struggles with believing she is capable of recovering, and she often finds herself berating herself for even minor mistakes she makes each day. She rationalizes her harshness toward herself by insisting that she needs to be tough on herself in order to improve and become a better student, athlete, friend, and daughter. At the same time, she is beginning to understand that her idea of "being better" does not have an end point, as she is constantly finding new ways in which she is "failing." She feels that nothing she does is ever good enough and that she might not be worthy of recovery.

While putting in effort to change your habits and improve yourself is vital to recovery, self-acceptance is equally as valuable. Chloe tends to be self-critical and struggles with believing she is even worthy of recovery. In order for her to make and sustain meaningful changes in her life, Chloe will need to explore how she can begin to accept herself. As discussed in previous chapters, acceptance and change are not opposite concepts that you must choose between, but rather two approaches that work together to help you move forward in your recovery and in life. While previous chapters focused on mechanisms of change, it's helpful to take time to consider the acceptance part of recovery. One of the most important aspects of acceptance in your recovery is self-acceptance. Self-acceptance is cultivated through self-efficacy, self-worth, and self-esteem, the building blocks for developing self-acceptance and self-love.

Self-Efficacy

Self-efficacy is your belief in your ability to succeed (Bandura 1977). Your sense of self-efficacy influences your behavior, motivation, thoughts, perception, approach to challenges and goals, and your psychological state and emotions. Having a strong sense of self-efficacy means that you believe you can succeed when faced with a challenge; having weak self-efficacy means you tend to be convinced you will fail even before tackling a situation.

How Is Improving Your Sense of Self-Efficacy Going to Benefit Your Recovery?

Self-efficacy gives you the motivation to face challenges and to achieve your goals. It builds up your confidence and desire to improve, because you feel worth it. It provides you with a sense of determination to do healthy and positive things for yourself rather than engage in self-destructive behaviors. Additionally, feeling efficacious in your recovery will help you view recovery positively and as something you can do successfully. It will help you recover from the slipups and disappointments that everyone experiences at times both in recovery and in life in general.

Fostering Self-Efficacy

Try, practice, and succeed. Avoidance robs us of the opportunity to try new things. Even though we may fail at first, by continuing to try, we will develop the skills needed and begin to achieve success. These "little victories" add up and help to increase our self-efficacy. We must not be ruled by a fear of failure. We must seek out opportunities to work on certain skills and behaviors, knowing that with practice they will get easier and easier, and we will start achieving positive results. Engaging in healthy behavior patterns will contribute to us feeling more confident in our ability to continue acting in this way. If Chloe, for example, completes her meal plan today—achieves this small victory—she'll feel more confident that she can do it tomorrow as well. While one meal may not spark instant change, the more Chloe complies with her meal plan, the more likely she will be to continue doing so. Her self-efficacy will also increase, and she'll gain confidence that she can resist her eating disordered urges and be successful in recovery.

As you try, practice, and succeed in recovery, it's important to monitor the comparisons we make in our minds. If Chloe is constantly comparing herself to someone who is fully recovered or to the idea of being perfect in recovery, she will feel that she is never doing well enough, and she will feel worse about herself and her ability to make progress. But, if she compares her efforts and positive actions to how she has done in the past, she is recognizing her progress and will likely feel more capable of making changes. All of these positive actions add up!

Think back to your work on SMART goals in chapter 6 (or go back to chapter 6 to learn about SMART goals if you have not completed that chapter yet). Create a list of one to three SMART goals you have for the next twenty-four hours. Make sure that items on this list are somewhat easy for you to accomplish. For example, your goal could be to stretch for fifteen minutes today or to leave your house without weighing yourself in the morning.

Goal 1: _____

_____

Goal 2: _____

_____

Goal 3: _____

_____

As you set subsequent goals, you want to build on your success by making your goals incrementally more difficult over time. For example, if you want to stretch for fifteen minutes three to five times per week by the end of the month, set intermediate goals, starting with once a week and adding days as you accomplish the lower level. By trying, practicing, and succeeding in recovery, you are setting yourself up for success by increasing your sense of self-efficacy.

Observe others succeed. Seeing people similar to yourself successfully perform tasks can boost your own sense of self-efficacy: *She's in the exact same position I'm in, and if she can do it, maybe I can too!* This is why group therapy, supported meal times with others with eating disorders, and recovery support groups can be so beneficial. When you see others improving in their behaviors, thinking, and attitudes, you are likely to view your own personal challenges as things that can be overcome. Your motivation to succeed is also increased as you see that recovery is possible.

To put this concept into action, interview two people whom you know in treatment or recovery and ask them to recall things they have successfully accomplished so far. Ask them how they were able to be successful in accomplishing these goals. Take notes to remind yourself that success is possible. Maybe you can learn from their efforts that helped them succeed!

1. Name: _____

What has she or he successfully accomplished in treatment or recovery? _____

_____

_____

_____

How was she or he able accomplish these goals? _____

_____

_____

_____

2. Name: _____

What has she or he successfully accomplished in treatment or recovery? _____

_____

_____

_____

How was she or he able accomplish these goals? _____

_____

_____

_____

Elicit encouragement from others. When others encourage us, we more easily overcome self-doubt and focus on giving our best efforts. Chloe, for example, struggles with following her meal plan, but she eats regularly with her family and friends, so she tells them both verbal and nonverbal ways they can be supportive and encouraging. Tell your friends, family, and treatment team which things are particularly challenging for you at the moment, and what the best forms of encouragement would be—as everyone responds differently to different forms of encouragement.

Let's begin by answering the following questions. From whom would hearing words of encouragement be helpful for you? Remember to consider your friends, family, religious or spiritual leaders, and treatment team members for this list.

1. _____

2. _____

3. _____

When are you likely to need encouragement? Are there regular times, like every mealtime? Are there special situations, like parties or social gatherings?

1. _____

2. _____

3. _____

What are the signs that others could notice that could signal that you are in need of encouragement?

1. _____

2. _____

3. _____

What specific forms of encouragement—particular phrases or special actions—do you find helpful?

1. _____

2. _____

3. _____

Now let's put it all together in the following chart. In the first column, list the individuals from your first list. In the second, identify when (situations, places, or events) you may need encouragement. In the third, name the signs you and others can observe that indicate you need encouragement. Finally, list the specific words or actions that would be meaningful and helpful.

See Chloe's responses as an example:

From Whom I Need Encouragement	When I May Need Encouragement	Signs I Need Encouragement	Effective Ways for This Person to Provide Encouragement
Mom	During meals	I'm playing with my food I'm taking a while to eat my meals	Validation such as "I know this is hard for you," and asking me how she can help in the moment
Coach	When I'm beating myself up for not performing my best	Not smiling Not enjoying myself at practice Being too serious	Pointing out what I'm doing well, and verbal reminders that I don't have to be perfect.

Now complete the chart yourself, and share it with those who can provide you with needed encouragement. This chart is also available at http://www.newharbinger.com/39348.

From Whom I Need Encouragement	When I May Need Encouragement	Signs I Need Encouragement	Effective Ways for This Person to Provide Encouragement

Manage your psychological responses. The way we react emotionally to situations also affects our self-efficacy. When we feel burdened by unpleasant emotions, we often perceive our ability to succeed as poor. By learning to tolerate and effectively deal with stress, anxiety, or a depressed mood in challenging situations, you can improve your sense of self-efficacy. You can work with your psychotherapist to determine which emotions impede your ability to feel capable of making recovery-focused choices and how you can react to them differently to make them less distressing for you (and see chapter 11 for more information on coping skills).

Listed below are some emotions that commonly cause difficulty. For each emotion, write down how you typically react to this emotion that can hinder your progress in recovery. Then identify alternate reactions that can make the emotions less distressing for you. Using Chloe's example as guidance, complete the table below. This chart is also available at http://www.newharbinger.com/39348.

Emotion and Current Reaction	Alternate Reaction
Anxiety. *When I'm anxious, I get overwhelmed and do whatever it takes to get the anxiety to go away as fast as possible.*	*When I get anxious, I can take several deep breaths to calm myself down. Then I can be more reflective about how I want to proceed.*
Anxiety.	
Shame.	
Sadness.	
Anger.	
_____ (insert emotion of your choice)	

Self-Worth

Self-worth is your own evaluation of how meaningful, valuable, worthy, and important you are as a whole or within particular areas of your life (Crocker and Park 2003). For many people, self-worth often fluctuates. We often use our accomplishments, failures, and others' interactions with us as indicators for how we "should" feel about ourselves. However, it is possible (and healthy) to feel a stable sense of self-worth because you are *you*, as who *you* are does not change in the face of external events. A stable sense of self-worth helps us to better deal with setbacks, as well as progress, effectively.

How Is Improving Your Sense of Self-Worth Going to Benefit Your Recovery?

Having a sense of self-worth means you value yourself. You view yourself as deserving of love, care, and happiness, and you see yourself as worthy of recovery. In essence, you believe that you deserve to be successful in your recovery efforts. If you do not believe this, you are not likely to put needed effort into making healthy and recovery-oriented choices for yourself. Furthermore, improving your self-worth will also allow you to handle disappointments in an adaptive way. Rather than taking disappointments personally and internalizing them, you will be more likely to separate yourself from those events and situations in your life. Your ability to deal with disappointments shifts from feeling negatively about yourself, and therefore punishing yourself, to feeling negatively about the disappointing situation and taking the necessary steps to change it.

Fostering Self-Worth

Engage in situations that foster self-worth. When do you feel important, valued, respected, and worthy? Make a list of events, situations, and roles that remind you of your inherent worth. These can be practically anything (e.g., going to religious services, practicing yoga, spending time with friends, taking care of animals, cleaning your room, writing poetry).

1. _____

2. _____

3. _____

4. _____

5. _____

Now, take a moment to jot down *when* and *where* you can begin to integrate each of the examples you listed above into your life. You may want to reference chapter 6 on setting SMART goals to help you begin these practices. It may also be helpful to brainstorm and discuss your ideas with your psychotherapist. Make the decision to engage in these circumstances as actively and as often as possible.

1. _____

2. _____

3. _____

4. _____

5. _____

Finally, try each of your ideas and reflect on how effective they are for you. Remember that you will likely need to do each activity more than once to feel a benefit. Use the space below to write about your experiences with these activities and how you feel about yourself as a result of engaging in them.

_____

_____

_____

_____

_____

Put yourself and your recovery first…be a little "selfish." First, let's take a moment to appreciate and understand why *selfish* is in quotation marks. Putting yourself first, acknowledging your worth, and viewing yourself as important is likely unfamiliar territory for you. It might feel selfish and indulgent to think and behave in ways that demonstrate that you are worthy of love, respect, care, and, most importantly, recovery. That is a common reaction, and those feelings are going to arise, especially in the beginning, when you are not yet comfortable feeling worthy or actively putting yourself in situations that make you feel good about yourself. Remember that those feelings are present because of your tendency to devalue yourself, which is familiar and perhaps comfortable. Acknowledge feeling selfish, and give yourself the permission to continue valuing yourself despite the discomfort. Eventually, as your self-worth improves, these feelings of selfishness will subside.

Anything you put ahead of your recovery you stand to lose. Without your recovery, you cannot have meaningful connections or relationships with others or yourself, nor can you fully engage in other aspects of your life, such as your career, education, spirituality, or service. Putting yourself and your recovery first does not mean that you cannot also participate in these other things; in fact, pursuing recovery, particularly on an outpatient basis, is most fulfilling when you are engaged in life *and* recovery. However, you need to be mindful of how life circumstances and your actions affect your recovery. By putting your recovery first, you may need to disengage from some activities or relationships that may hinder your progress. For example, you may need to take a break from social media, tell your boss you can no longer take extra shifts, or create some distance from friends who may be actively engaging in their eating disorders. While this may feel uncomfortable at first, putting yourself and your recovery first is an important way to begin improving your self-worth.

Where in your recovery do you feel you need to put yourself first more often?

_____

_____

_____

What gets in the way of you putting yourself first?

_____

_____

_____

What are some ways you might start putting yourself first in these areas of your recovery?

_____

_____

_____

Replace your negative core beliefs. Core beliefs are ideas about ourselves, others, and the world around us that we hold to be true. They impact the way we feel, behave, and think about ourselves, our relationships, and life. What are your beliefs about your worthiness, value, and importance to others? Many of us have negative beliefs, such as *I am not worth recovery, I am a burden to everyone,* and *I'm incompetent and selfish.* Take some time to identify the negative core beliefs you have about yourself and list them on the next page.

- _____
- _____
- _____
- _____
- _____

That was likely relatively easy. Now for the more difficult part: compile a list of your positive core beliefs. You may not necessarily be able to take a negative core belief and rephrase it to be a positive one. Core beliefs take time to change. Instead, make a list of positive beliefs that you also have or can believe for yourself that may be unrelated to your negative beliefs. Remember to challenge your black-and-white thinking (i.e., thinking that things are either all negative or all positive); you can believe something negative about yourself *and* also something else positive at the same time. Because you are likely hyper-focused on your negative core beliefs, it may be helpful to work with your psychotherapist, friends, or family to begin this new list. For example, *I am smart, I must be strong to have come this far in recovery,* and *I'm working hard in recovery.*

- _____
- _____
- _____
- _____
- _____

When you catch yourself thinking one of your negative core beliefs, try to acknowledge that thought and choose a positive core belief to think about instead. This is easier said than done. You may want to repeat the positive core belief several times, or you may want to place visual reminders of your positive core beliefs around you (e.g., at your desk, in your car). Your negative core beliefs may not simply go away, but by combating them with positive beliefs you can begin to balance out your view of yourself.

Self-Esteem

Self-esteem is your evaluation of how you feel about yourself (Rosenberg 1965). It is not inherent; it must be developed. Your experiences, social and familial interactions, childhood, and reactions to successes and failures all impact your development of self-esteem. Low self-esteem, a common feature among individuals with anorexia, can contribute to you blaming yourself for external events. Feeling at fault creates a sense of self-hate and tends to lead to feeling as if you need to be punished, which can fuel your eating disorder. If you feel you are deserving of punishment, you are more likely to believe statements like *I deserve to have an eating disorder, I don't deserve to recover,* or *I need to purge to punish myself.* If you have feelings of self-hate, you are not going to take care of your physical, mental, emotional, and social well-being. Additionally, as humans, we are likely to remember, interpret, and magnify cues that match our self-concept. When your self-esteem is low, you are more likely to remember the one time when you were ignored and forget the multiple times you were not ignored.

How Is Improving Your Self-Esteem Going to Benefit Your Recovery?

Just as negative self-esteem leads you to treat yourself poorly, if you view yourself in a positive light you are likely to want to treat yourself well, take positive steps to improve your overall health, and make strides in your recovery. Additionally, you are more likely to interact with others in ways that elicit positive responses. You are also more likely to be able to focus on the positive social interactions and brush off the negative ones, which will help continue your process of improving and maintaining a healthy and positive sense of self-esteem and aid in your recovery.

Fostering Self-Esteem

Define your "self" in various domains. Often a low sense of self-esteem comes from having a narrow sense of self or few areas in which we feel effective or worthy (Crocker and Park 2003). When we place our value and esteem in only a few domains, we are at greater risk for a decreased sense of self-esteem. For example, suppose you identify as being a student, a daughter, and an athlete. What happens to your sense of self if you get a bad grade, fight with your parents, and acquire an injury that sidelines you for several weeks? Your self-esteem likely suffers because you have "failed" in the only three ways by which you define yourself. Now, let's expand our definition of your self to include other roles, values, and sources of identity—your emotional self, physical self, spiritual self, social self, relational self, professional self, educational self, cultural self, sexual self, and recreational self. The more ways you identify and value yourself, the more stable your self-esteem is in relation to external events.

Chapter 9 provides more information and exercises related to developing your sense of self and identity. However, to get you started defining your self in various domains, create a list of ten things that are important to you. These can be anything (family, pets, work, or activities you enjoy). We will come back to this list later on in chapter 9.

1. _____

2. _____

3. _____

4. _____

5. _____

6. _____

7. _____

8. _____

9. _____

10. _____

Identify and acknowledge your positive qualities. Using your newly expanded sense of self, take some time to recognize your positive attributes within each domain. As you do this, you may find yourself discounting certain areas in which you are not perfect. For example, you may think *I'm a good friend, but I isolate a lot so I can't be that good of a friend,* or *I am a capable and loving mother, but I would be better if I spent more time with my kids on the weekends.* This is common among individuals with anorexia, who often struggle with perfectionism. When you find yourself qualifying a positive quality with a "but I could be better" type of comment, take notice, stop, and correct it. Instead of saying, *I am caring toward others, but I think about myself too much sometimes,* try *Although I think about myself too much sometimes, I am also caring toward others.* Two things that may seem to be opposites can be simultaneously true. One perceived negative quality does not cancel out one positive quality. Complete the following activity to help you practice.

First, take some time to make a list of the positive qualities you believe you possess—talents, achievements, personality traits, contributions to groups or society, roles you play (e.g., sister or friend), strengths, things you enjoy, or goals and dreams you have. You can also consider what others would say your positive qualities are or consult with your treatment team, friends, and family members to help you create this list.

- _____
- _____
- _____
- _____
- _____

Now, notice your reactions as you read these positive qualities. For some of you, you may feel quite confident and rarely doubt or dismiss these positive qualities. For others, however, you may have the initial reaction of *But I'm not that good at it*, *But I could be better*, or *But others are so much better than I am*. When these reactions or thoughts come up, try to challenge yourself to appreciate the positive aspects of yourself without allowing self-doubt or comparisons to negate them. Fill in the first part of each sentence below with something you feel inhibits you from being able to say something fully positive about yourself. Then, complete the second part with something positive about yourself that is true regardless of what you wrote in the first blank. Look at Chloe's statements:

Although I do not follow my meal plan perfectly every day, I am also doing the best I can in my recovery.

Although I become very irritable with my parents when I'm at home, I also love them and am trying my best to form positive relationships with them.

Although I make mistakes, I am also a good person who is worthy of recovery.

Now try some of your own:

Although I _____,

I also _____.

Although I _____,

I also _____.

Although I _____,

I also _____.

Practice positive affirmations. Positive affirmations—short, positive things about yourself, like *I am worthy of recovery*— are deceptively simple. They may seem simple, but changing the way we talk to ourselves can have profound effects on how we view and treat ourselves. When choosing positive affirmations, it is important that you select things that are realistic and believable, even if you do not believe them in the moment. If they are not realistic at all, you are more likely to dismiss them. It is also important to avoid affirmations that compare you to others, as the positive feeling is not based on a universal truth about you. Try to focus on affirmations that remind you of your innate worth and validate your positive qualities. Chloe, for example, may choose *I am worthy of recovery*, *Making mistakes does not make me a bad person*, and *I'm doing the best I can right now*.

Creating positive affirmations is often a difficult task when you are simply prompted to "say something positive to yourself." Write your responses to the following questions to help jumpstart your list. You can also use your statements from the previous exercise. Before you write your responses, take a look at Chloe's responses for some guidance.

What things in my life are most important to me?

Chloe: *I care very much about being a good friend, daughter, student, and athlete. I value connection, family, knowledge, and growth.*

You: _____

_____

_____

What do I want for myself in life?

Chloe: *I want to live a fulfilling life in accordance with my values. I want to be content and able to handle adversity. I want to be a good role model and an inspiration to others.*

You: _____

_____

_____

What are some negative scripts I often replay in my head that could use some countering?

Chloe: *I spend a lot of time thinking about and hating myself for little mistakes that I make. I also consistently tell myself that I'm never going to recover, that I'm not doing enough in my recovery, and that I'm not worthy of recovering. My thoughts also tend to focus on my difficulty connecting to others.*

You: _____

_____

_____

Using the ideas from these reflections, write some positive affirmations that you believe and that are specific to you. You can look at Chloe's examples for how to take your answers to the above questions and turn them into positive affirmations.

- *I am good enough.*

- *I deserve to recover.*

- *I am intelligent. I am unique. And I matter.*

- *I'm doing the best I can.*

- *I'm a good friend, especially when I am not restricting myself both in terms of my eating disorder and in my relationships.*

- *I can do hard things.*

Now, write yours below.

- _____

- _____

- _____

- _____

- _____

Post your positive affirmations in places where you will see them on a daily basis. Repeat them frequently.

Stop comparing yourself to others. Avoiding comparisons is important not only in positive affirmations—it is something you should eliminate entirely from your life. Because we live in a society driven by comparison (you cannot watch television or read a magazine without seeing taglines encouraging you to be smarter or thinner or prettier than others), eliminating comparison will require constant awareness and conscious efforts. As Theodore Roosevelt is often quoted as saying, "Comparison is the thief of joy." When we compare ourselves to others, we create an atmosphere and mind-set of constant competition. We focus so much of our time on "winning" that we forget to focus on our true selves, our values, our well-being, and our happiness. By choosing to recognize and let go of comparisons, you can make room for feeling good about yourself.

The first step in decreasing self-comparison is to recognize when you are doing it. Pay attention and be mindful. In the moment, when you catch yourself comparing yourself to others, remind yourself that comparisons are not helpful and try to reframe your view of yourself. For example, if you catch yourself thinking, *She is thinner than I am*, reframe your thought: *I am working on taking care of me and accepting my body as it is.* It may be helpful to log your self-comparisons so you can track how often and what types of comparisons are being made. Use the chart below to track and reframe your self-comparisons. This chart is also available at http://www.newharbinger.com/39348.

Date	Time	Self-Comparison	Reframe
8/26	4 p.m.	*She is thinner than I am.*	*I'm working on taking care of and accepting my body as it is.*

Tracking your comparisons will not only allow you to see what types you are making, the habit of writing them down will encourage you to notice them when they occur. It will be less likely that such comparisons will slide through your consciousness, eating away at your self-esteem, without being noticed and changed.

Practice self-care. Engaging in activities that you enjoy and taking care of your physical, emotional, psychological, social, and spiritual self positively affects your self-esteem. Whereas the earlier techniques have taken the approach of "improve your self-esteem, and you will then treat yourself better as a result," self-care works in the opposite direction. It works because the relationship between improving your self-esteem and taking care of yourself is cyclical; by improving in one area, you improve the other. By taking care of yourself, you create a routine of self-respect and self-worth. While it may feel forced in the beginning, the more you treat yourself as someone who has value and positive qualities, the more you will internalize these actions. As self-care is such an important element to the recovery process, an entire chapter is dedicated to this topic later (chapter 11).

Self-Acceptance

Self-acceptance means you are able to embrace your whole and authentic self, both the positive aspects on which you base your self-esteem and all of your imperfections, weaknesses, and limitations. However, accepting yourself while simultaneously knowing you also need to change aspects of your behavior, attitude, and ways of thinking may seem contradictory. You may think, *If I'm going to accept myself as I am, how can I also want to change myself?* To answer, consider this: *How can I improve myself if I do not value, care about, or believe in myself enough to do so?* Note that we are acknowledging the need to change eating disordered behaviors, attitudes, and thoughts, but not *you,* as you are much more than these behaviors, attitudes, and thoughts. Also, self-acceptance does not mean settling with where you are in life or in your recovery; in addition to acknowledging and embracing aspects of yourself that you may deem as "negative," self-acceptance also involves feeling confident in your ability to overcome obstacles (self-efficacy); feeling worthy, valuable, and important enough to try (self-worth); and feeling positively about yourself in various areas (self-esteem).

How Is Cultivating Self-Acceptance Going to Benefit Your Recovery?

In recovery, your journey of self-acceptance includes body acceptance (both where your body is currently in terms of weight, size, and shape and, if it is not at its natural set point, where your body is meant to be), emotional acceptance (acknowledging and experiencing all emotions, as all of your emotions are valid), and cognitive acceptance (acknowledging that your mind may have eating disordered thoughts, but you do not have to act on them). Further, it involves accepting where you are in your recovery journey, as well as accepting where you are in your life, which may be different from where you would like to be at this point in your life. Self-acceptance includes accepting that you indeed have an eating disorder and the physical, psychological, social, and emotional side effects that have accompanied it. It is accepting that you are human and need food to live. Ultimately, it is the process of feeling at peace with yourself.

Fostering Self-Acceptance

Be vulnerable and authentic. "Authenticity is the daily practice of letting go of who we think we're supposed to be and embracing who we are" (Brown 2010, 50). To be authentic is to be real. This practice of authenticity requires a significant amount of courage, because being our true selves involves being vulnerable. Vulnerability is scary, and you have likely used your eating disorder to hide a large portion of yourself. By restricting food, you restrict your life and your experience of emotions (both uncomfortable and pleasurable feelings), connections with others, and a sense of identity. To commit to being authentic means to practice peeling away the layers of protection your eating disorder has provided and to sit with the discomfort of being raw and vulnerable. By doing so, you are making steps toward self-acceptance, as you cannot accept your true and whole self unless you make that holistic version of yourself available and seen.

Practice self-compassion. In order to accept yourself, you need to practice being compassionate toward yourself. This means making efforts to be kind and empathic to yourself and forgiving yourself for mistakes you have made and will continue to make. What if you were kind, empathic, and compassionate toward yourself rather than beating yourself up for perceived failures? Remember that if recovery were an easy process, you would have already done it! In practicing self-compassion, you learn to validate yourself and your emotions. You learn to accept yourself as a whole person who has both strengths and weaknesses.

To begin practicing self-compassion, try writing letters to yourself. First, write a letter to your childhood self. What would you want to say to this version of yourself? What do you want to apologize for? What do you want to forgive and validate for your younger self? Take a look at what Chloe wrote for guidance.

Dear Past Self,

I am sorry that I expected so much from you. You were just a little kid and needed help from others. I should not have judged you for failing to meet my perfectionistic expectations.

_____

_____

_____

_____

_____

_____

_____

_____

Next, write a letter to your future self (yourself in five or ten years). What would you want to say to this version of yourself? What types of commitments or assurances do you want to make to your future self? What are your hopes for your future self?

Dear Future Self,

You have worked so hard in life that you deserve what you have accomplished. Despite questioning yourself, you stuck through the hard times and now have a meaningful life full of wonderful things.

_____

_____

_____

_____

_____

_____

_____

Now, write a letter from your future self back to your current self. What do you envision your future self would hope your current self feels, thinks, believes, and does? What do you forgive your current self for?

Dear Current Self,

Hang in there. I know you want what is best for us even though it is difficult at times to keep moving toward recovery. You are stronger than you think and recovery is worth it, if you can just keep going. I believe in you.

_____

_____

_____

_____

_____

_____

_____

Take some time to reflect on these letters. When were you most compassionate? When could you have provided more compassion for yourself? What parts of yourself are you having difficulty accepting?

_____

_____

_____

_____

_____

Cultivate body acceptance. While your physical self is just a small portion of who you are, accepting your body is an important aspect of self-acceptance, particularly for those in recovery from an eating disorder. Because individuals with anorexia struggle with a distorted body image, body acceptance is of particular importance and difficulty. When you are entrenched in your eating disorder, you experience a disconnection from your body. Perhaps you have felt a strong hatred toward your body or felt as if your body was betraying you.

The first step to move from this disconnection is through a cognitive shift that allows you to appreciate all parts of your body, everything from your thighs and stomach to your hair and feet. For example, *I appreciate my arms.* Appreciating is simply acknowledging that you are thankful to have that body part as opposed to not having it. Once you can appreciate the fact that you have these parts of your body, you can move into a logical frame of mind whereby you recognize the functionality of each part of your body. For example, *I appreciate my legs; they allow me to walk.* Acknowledging a logical reason for why you appreciate your body parts is an important step in body acceptance, as it helps you fight off negative body image thoughts (*Yes, I perceive my thighs as being fat, but my thighs help me walk and run and therefore I appreciate that I have them.*). The next step is to accept each part of your body. *I appreciate my hips. They allow me to sit and dance. Today, I accept my hips as they are.* Acceptance moves beyond the logical reasons as to why you appreciate your body parts and leads you to accepting them as they are, regardless of your feelings toward them.

Once you've accepted the parts of your body as they are, you can begin to find aspects you like (and, eventually, love) about them outside of their biological functions. *Today, I like my face, shoulders, and toes. Today, I love my butt, chest, and mouth.* Liking or loving your body parts is not a sign of arrogance, though society often makes us feel that it is wrong to love our bodies. Your body is an important part of who you are, and practicing acceptance of it will help you practice self-acceptance. To help you get started, complete the exercise below.

In the first part, describe where you currently stand with each body part. Using the verbs "appreciate," "accept," "like," and "love," fill in the first blank for each sentence. If you feel that none of these four verbs reflect your feelings or relationship with a specific body part, feel free to use your own language. Just remember to focus on neutral or positive terms. Then, write a reason why you appreciate, accept, like, or love that body part. Remember that this can be logical (its biological purpose and function) or it can be more emotional and perceptive in nature (*It is beautifully shaped,* or *They are strong and help me accomplish my goals.*). Take time to reflect on your own and with your psychotherapist about areas where you are doing well with accepting, liking, and loving the parts of your body, and where you are having difficulty.

Today, I _____ my hair because _____

_____.

Today, I _____ my eyes because _____

_____.

Today, I _____ my nose because _____

_____.

Today, I _____ my ears because _____

_____.

Today, I _____ my neck because _____

_____.

Today, I _____ my shoulders because _____

_____.

Today, I _____ my arms because _____

_____.

Today, I _____ my hands because _____

_____.

Today, I _____ my chest/breasts because _____

_____.

Today, I _____ my stomach because _____

_____.

Today, I _____ my hips because _____

_____.

Today, I _____ my legs because _____

_____.

Today, I _____ my feet because _____

_____.

Let go of perfectionism. First, let's take a moment to define what perfectionism is and is not. Perfectionism is not the same as determination, motivation, enthusiasm, achievement, self-improvement, or trying to do your best. Instead, *perfectionism* is constantly striving for an unattainable goal, as perfection simply does not exist. The belief that if you appear and feel perfect you can avoid judgment and shame is an illusion, because the nature of perfectionism is that you will never be satisfied. There will always be some way to be better or to improve.

By pursuing perfection, you are essentially setting yourself up for *more* judgment and shame, as you are pursuing something that does not exist. You will lose this battle and never feel good enough, blaming yourself for not achieving something that is actually impossible. What if you decided to acknowledge and embrace your imperfections? What if you stopped focusing on how you think others perceive you and started focusing on what you want for yourself? It is healthy and normal to want to improve and grow as a person.

Take a step back and think about your motivations for being in recovery. If you find that you want to "be better" because doing so would make you more desirable to and accepted by others, or because it would appease the fear that others (or you) will negatively judge you, you are likely relying on perfectionism. However, if you want to "be better" because the improvement is congruent with what you truly value in life, you are likely relying on a healthy sense of self-growth.

Let's take a moment to examine the ways perfectionism plays a role in your life. Think of the areas of your life in which you tend to be most perfectionistic, and use the questions below as guidance for reflection.

What are the advantages of your perfectionism?

_____

_____

_____

In what ways is your perfectionism getting in the way of you living a values-focused life (In other words, how are you putting your pursuit of perfection ahead of your relationships or your health, and, as a result, not living authentically because you are putting on a façade to hide imperfections)?

_____

_____

_____

What are some ways you can devote less energy to perfectionism and more energy toward pursing your values?

_____

_____

_____

It Takes Time

The journey toward self-acceptance is not easy, and it is certainly not quick. Each of the topics and skills we discussed throughout this chapter will take time to develop. In fact, self-acceptance is a lifelong journey for most of us. It is a journey in which we have to consistently notice our minds—our thoughts and feelings about ourselves—and reorient ourselves to our values, reframing unhelpful thoughts and processing the emotions that come up for us.

Journaling Pages

In this chapter, we discussed the concepts of self-efficacy, self-worth, self-esteem, and self-acceptance, as well as the ways each of these self-concepts influences recovery from anorexia. We walked you through numerous exercises that explore who you are and who you want to be, helping you to build confidence, to work toward feeling good about your self, and to accept your strengths and weaknesses, all of which are vital to long-term recovery. This chapter may have been difficult, because anorexia often robs you of your former identity. As you recover from anorexia, you need to get back in touch with your healthy identity or form a new, post-anorexia self. Take some time to reflect on what it was like to complete the exercises in this chapter. In your own words, where do you feel you stand in terms of your self-efficacy, your self-worth, your self-esteem, and your self-acceptance? Where do you hope to be in the next year? Consider sharing your thoughts with your psychotherapist.

_____

_____

_____

_____

_____

_____

_____

_____

_____

_____

_____

_____

Defining Yourself Without Your Eating Disorder

The thing that is really hard, and really amazing, is giving up on being perfect and beginning the work of becoming yourself.

—Anna Quindlen

Meet Rachel

Rachel is a single mother who has been struggling with anorexia for several years. Due to her declining physical health, she and her two children moved into her parents' house last year. In the midst of her eating disorder, she found this arrangement helpful, as she worried less about leaving her children to go to the emergency room or her various appointments throughout the week. Now in her recovery, however, Rachel finds herself having a difficult time reestablishing her identity as a responsible mother and caregiver. She feels stuck in her role as "the sick one" and struggles with falling back into her previous patterns of being overly dependent on her parents for emotional and financial support. While she knows that she wants to establish her identity outside of her eating disorder, she is also scared about being independent again.

In chapter 8, we began the discussion of expanding your sense of self as a means of improving your self-esteem. This is not an easy task, especially for individuals recovering from anorexia. Having an eating disorder is an all-consuming experience, and you have likely developed a strong sense of identity related to it. As with Rachel, it is common to feel that you are "the sick one," "the anorexic," or "the thin one." If you have defined yourself in terms of your eating disorder for a significant period of time, you may feel a sense of confusion or ambivalence about to how to expand your definition of yourself. Let's take some time to reflect on what it means to expand and improve your sense of identity and take steps to help you do so.

Who Am I If I'm Not the Sick One?

As you continue your journey in recovery, you may find yourself clinging to or missing your eating disorder as a way to identify yourself. Perhaps you do not know who you are outside of being someone with an eating disorder. In the depths of your eating disorder, you may have felt that being the sick one was your sole source of identity. Now in recovery, you may be experiencing difficulty discovering and establishing who you are. As discussed in chapter 5, letting go of your eating disorder can involve a grieving process, and part of this process can include the sense that you are losing part of your identity. Take some time to reflect on ways your eating disorder has impacted your sense of self with the prompts below.

What does being the sick one, the anorexic, or the thin one mean in your life?

Rachel: *Being the sick one means that I don't have to take responsibility for as many things. People do not expect as much of me.*

You: _____

_____

_____

What fears do you have in giving up that part of your identity?

Rachel: *I don't know who or what I am outside of my eating disorder. I'm afraid that I don't know what my life would look like if I didn't have an eating disorder.*

You: _____

_____

_____

What needs may be unmet for you if others do not identify you as being sick?

Rachel: *Specifically, my parents might not be so willing to take care of my kids while I attend therapy appointments. In general, I might not get any attention from others.*

You: _____

_____

_____

How may you have been using your eating disorder as a way to feel a sense of self?

Rachel: *I always felt special growing up, because I was the thin one in the family. If I'm no longer the thinnest, then what makes me special?*

You: _____

_____

_____

What parts of your identity and yourself have you been avoiding by acting on your eating disorder?

Rachel: *I have always been fairly shy being around other people. My eating disorder has given me an excuse not to socialize. Even though I want to have friends, I won't have an excuse not to spend time with them anymore.*

You: _____

_____

_____

Now, let's take these reflections a step further. In what ways can you get your needs met without being sick? How do you meet these needs for others who are not sick? What new roles can you fulfill that can help you move away from being the sick one? Write your responses in the space below.

Rachel: *If I no longer had my eating disorder, I could get positive attention from others rather than them always worrying about me because I'm so thin. I find it more gratifying to spend time with friends who are not sick, so I imagine this would be the same for my friends. In the past, my children have been invited on playdates, but I have avoided them because of my social anxiety. I could accept some of these invitations and begin working on strengthening my role as a mother and meet new people in the process.*

You: _____

_____

_____

_____

_____

Using Your Values

Who are you? This is a simple question that has a complex answer, as what makes up a person is a complicated concept. You play different roles; you have biological, cultural, and genetic influences that impact who you are; you have a variety of characteristics and personality traits that make up *you*. We will get to these concrete ways of defining your identity in the next section, but first, let's take a moment to reflect on who you are and who you want to be in an unstructured format. Write your responses to the questions below to help you begin to formulate an idea of the person you are and would like to be outside of your eating disorder.

1.   Using your values (see chapter 6) as a guide, in what ways would you like to be defined by yourself and others? What parts of you would you like to be most salient? What parts would you like to be less important in the definition of you? How do these ideas compare to your current view of what makes up your identity?

Rachel: *I want people to see me as a good mother, daughter, and friend. I want to believe that I am capable of fulfilling my responsibilities toward my children. I don't want other people to have to take care of my kids because I'm too tired or because I'm not even around—if I'm at the hospital or in treatment appointments. This is different from how things are currently. Right now, others don't see me as able to take care of myself or my kids. This makes me feel worthless, which fuels me to continue my eating disorder.*

You: _____

_____

_____

_____

2.   How do you want others to remember you? Thinking into the future, for example, what would you like to be included in your eulogy (the speech of praise for someone who has died) or on your epitaph (a short text honoring someone who has passed away)?

Rachel: *I want people to remember me as someone who would do anything for her kids, someone who was always there at her kids' school and sports events, supporting them. I want my kids to feel loved. I want them to feel that I was always there for them. I want my friends to remember me similarly and be able to recall many good times that we had together. I would like people to speak about my commitment to my faith and my love of music and animals.*

You: _____

_____

_____

_____

3.   What would be written or said now versus what you would like to be written or said?

Rachel: *Now, people would probably recall me as someone whose life was filled with sickness and not lived to its fullest. People would probably say that they feel bad for my kids, because their mother was not available for them. They might even be glad that I finally succumbed to my illness, because I was no longer suffering.*

You: _____

_____

_____

_____

Domains of Identity

In chapter 8 we began discussing the importance of expanding your identity as a means of improving your self-esteem. Let's take some time to delve deeper into this topic and discuss what it means to have a strong and multifaceted sense of identity. Your identity is composed of the characteristics by which you define yourself. Having a strong sense of identity means you feel connected to the roles, experiences, and characteristics that define you; you feel like you know who you are. Having a multifaceted sense of identity means you have many ways in which you define yourself. While your current sense of identity may be narrow and heavily focused on being someone in recovery from an eating disorder, it is important to establish other characteristics of yourself. It may feel important to you that part of your identity is being someone in recovery from anorexia; that is normal and healthy, and it very much informs your perceptions, attitudes, thoughts, behaviors, and interactions. However, it is equally important to remember that you are not *only* a person in recovery. In order to move past your eating disorder, you need to begin to conceptualize yourself as more than your illness.

In chapter 8, several domains by which you can hold a sense of identity were listed (your emotional self, physical self, spiritual self, social self, relational self, professional self, educational self, cultural self, sexual self, and recreational self). To help you begin to brainstorm ways in which you identify yourself, complete the diagram on the next page. In the center, we start with "my identity." Then, branching off and in relation to your identity, consider the roles, experiences, and values you connect with within each domain listed above. Fill in each bubble, adding more, if needed, until you feel like the diagram captures the true essence of who you are. When you are finished, take a moment to appreciate how unique you are, with all the roles you play in life, and all the domains you have to help improve your self-efficacy, self-worth, and self-esteem. Before completing your own diagram, take a look at Rachel's as an example. The blank diagram is also available at http://www.newharbinger.com/39348.

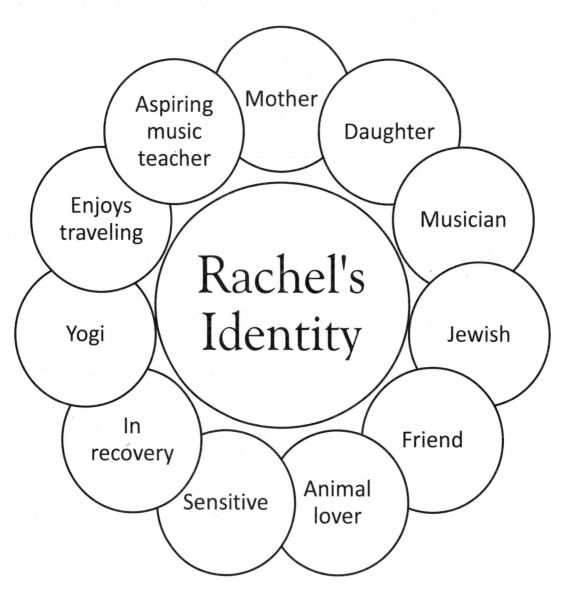

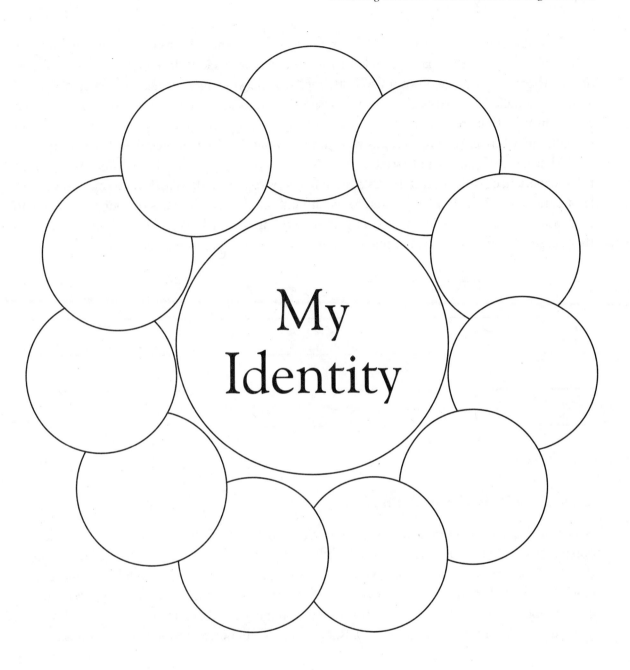

Now that you have completed the exercise, let's take some time to reflect on the following points. You can use the space provided to write down your ideas. It would also be helpful to discuss these reflections with your psychotherapist, as developing a strong, multifaceted sense of identity is challenging. Also, there may be aspects of your identity that seem unrelated to your eating disorder that are impacting your recovery (e.g., being confused or uncomfortable with your sexuality may hinder your recovery as you gain weight and become more physically mature).

What parts of your identity were easy for you to write down and acknowledge? With which roles, experiences, and characteristics do you feel most connected? With which ones do you feel least connected? Which domains were more difficult for you? What parts of your self elicited an unpleasant emotional response (e.g., anger, anxiety, discomfort)? What is it about those parts that caused you to have an emotional reaction?

_____

_____

_____

_____

_____

Compare and Contrast

Now that you have considered both your identity tied to your eating disorder and your identity outside of your eating disorder, it's worthwhile to create a visual representation of the changes that have occurred so far in your recovery and the changes that you would still like to see. Complete the following pie charts, dividing the circles into the parts of your identity with which you previously felt and now feel most connected, using bigger proportions to represent those you feel are most descriptive of your identity. Rachel's ideas will be presented first as examples.

What Made Up Your Identity in the Midst of Your Eating Disorder?

In the first pie chart, indicate your identity while you were actively engaging in your eating disorder. Then, in the space below, take a moment to reflect on your thoughts, feelings, and reactions to your pie chart. Was anything about your pie chart surprising? Is your chart split in equal parts, or do you find your identity is made up more of certain domains? Did you have a hard time coming up with areas of your identity not related to your eating disorder? Are you satisfied or dissatisfied with how much of your identity is wrapped up in the eating disorder? This exercise is also available at http://www.newharbinger.com/39348.

Rachel's Identity During Her Eating Disorder

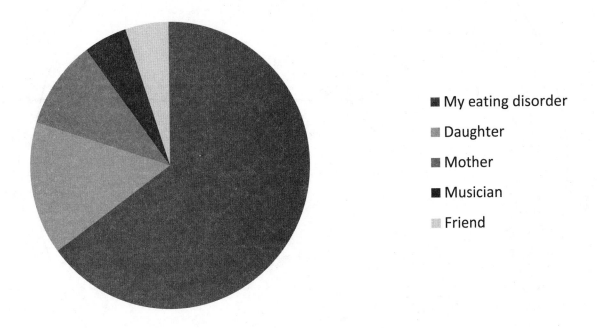

When I was actively engaging in my eating disorder, it consumed my identity. I didn't really know or care to know too much of who I was outside of it. I was also largely defined by my dependence on my parents and very little by my role as a mother, since my parents had taken over much of that responsibility. I wanted to be a friend and an active musician, but my mental and physical health kept me away from those parts of myself.

Your Identity During Your Eating Disorder

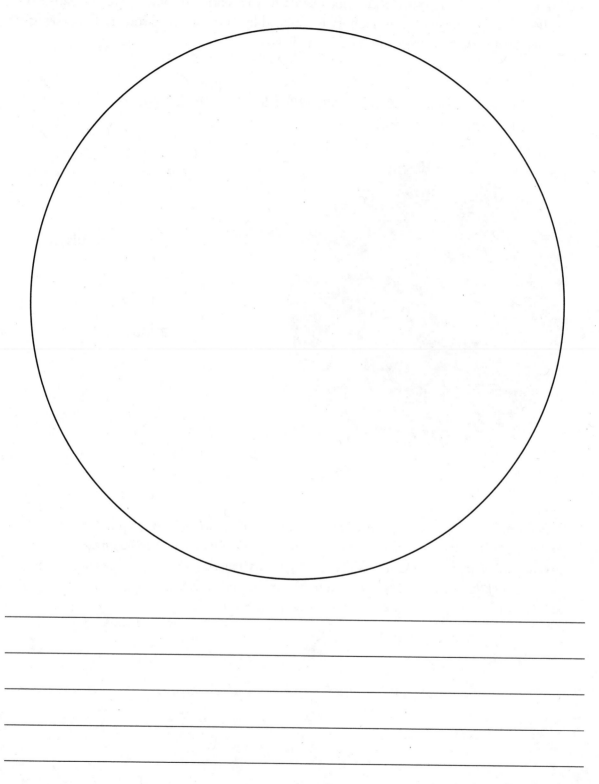

What Makes Up Your Identity Right Now?

In this second pie chart, indicate your identity as you currently describe yourself. Then, in the space below, take a moment to reflect on your thoughts, feelings, and reactions to your pie chart. What changes between the first and second charts stand out for you? Are the parts that make up your identity more equally distributed in the chart? Are you more or less satisfied with how your new chart appears?

Rachel's Identity Now

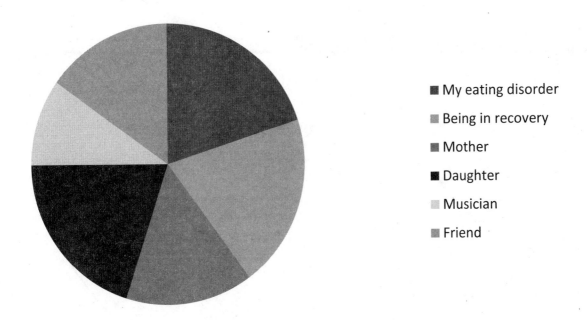

■ My eating disorder

■ Being in recovery

■ Mother

■ Daughter

■ Musician

■ Friend

Right now, a good portion of my identity is still centered around my eating disorder. However, I'm happy that the sick role in my identity has decreased and my connection with my recovery is now an equally prominent part of who I am. I still see myself as more of a daughter than a mother, which is related to my struggle with regaining my independence from my parents. I'm also able to enjoy music and be a mother a little more than when I was active in my eating disorder, but I still have a lot of room to grow in those areas.

Your Identity Now

_____

_____

_____

_____

_____

How Do You Want to Define Your Identity in the Future?

In this last pie chart, indicate how you would like your identity to be represented in the future. In the space below, take a moment to reflect on your thoughts, feelings, and reactions to your pie chart. How do all three of your charts compare? What was it like to progress from one chart to the next? How do you feel about this last chart? Do you think it is possible to achieve?

Rachel's Identity in the Future

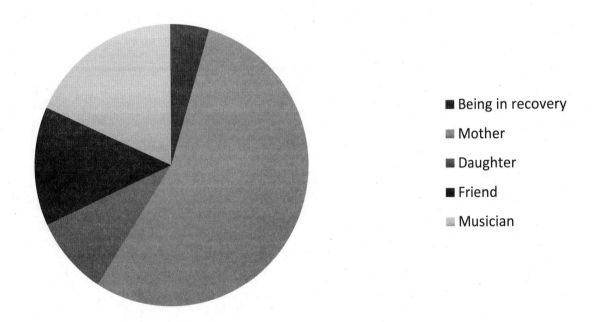

Being a mother is the most important thing to me, so I really want that to occupy most of my time, energy, and identity in the future. I want being in recovery to still be a part of me, but I don't want it to be the focus of my life. Similarly, I want to be a good daughter, but I want to gain independence from my parents. I hope to enjoy my passion for music more and be a better friend.

Your Identity in the Future

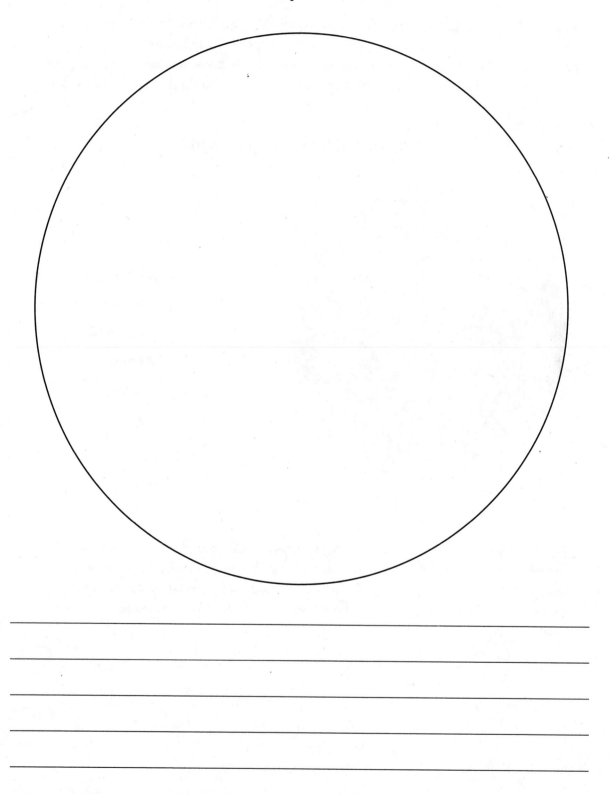

_____

_____

_____

_____

_____

Importance of Others in Our Sense of Identity

Humans are social beings. We do not live in isolation, but as part of one or more communities. Therefore, others in our life play an important role in our sense of identity. We gain information about who we are as individuals from our interactions and experiences with others. We become parts of groups (our family, social circles, clubs, religious organizations, sports teams) with which we learn to identify. We also learn about ourselves through others; we make judgments and evaluations of others' behaviors, attitudes, and personality characteristics to help us determine which of those we would like (and would not like) to see in ourselves (Baumeister and Leary 1995). As our identity forms, we try on different hats, trying out different ways of being to find what feels right and true to us.

In recovery, you may have difficulty developing your sense of identity outside your eating disorder because of the isolation your eating disorder caused psychologically, physically, emotionally, and socially. When we are isolated, we struggle to feel that we belong. Belonging to something greater than ourselves is a natural desire for most people. In order to belong, however, we need first to accept ourselves as we are and be authentic across settings and roles. Many people look at a situation and think, *How do I have to change in order to fit in* This is not belonging. Belonging is being true to yourself and thinking, *What situations fit with who I am?*

> *Because this yearning [to belong] is so primal, we often try to acquire it by fitting in and by seeking approval, which are not only hollow substitutes for belonging, but often barriers to it. Because true belonging only happens when we present our authentic, imperfect selves to the world, our sense of belonging can never be greater than our level of self-acceptance. (Brown 2010, 26)*

Take some time to reflect on this quote from Brené Brown's *The Gifts of Imperfection* using these questions as a starting point: Where do you feel you belong? What are some ways in which you wish you felt that you belonged to something greater (a social circle, a religious practice, a family system, or another group)? How can you practice authenticity to help gain a sense of belonging? How can you actively engage yourself in situations and with others to learn about yourself and to develop a sense of where you belong?

_____

_____

_____

_____

_____

As this chapter highlights, understanding and connecting with your identity is a difficult process. Sometimes you can intellectually list all of the roles, experiences, and characteristics that define who you are but still struggle to feel like that is enough. It is important to explore such feelings of inadequacy with your psychotherapist to help you gain insight into what is hindering you from feeling like the parts of your identity you listed in the above sections are sufficient in replacing the eating disordered part of your identity. Remember that identity formation and connection is a challenging process for everyone, especially for those who have had their identity disrupted by and periodically defined by an eating disorder.

Journaling Pages

In this chapter, we discussed the importance of defining yourself outside of your eating disorder and the challenges in giving up your role as the sick one. We also addressed various domains in which to develop your identity, as well as the role others play in your sense of self. Take some time to reflect on who you are outside of your eating disorder. What are the prominent values that guide who you want to become? What are some ways that you can start to move toward becoming the person you want to be? It may be helpful to talk with your psychotherapist about your thoughts.

_____

_____

_____

_____

_____

_____

_____

_____

_____

_____

Chapter 10

Building Your Social Network

People assume when you're swimming in a river you are supposed to know which way you are going, and I guess some of the time that is true, but there are certain currents that are very strong, and it's when we are in those currents we need somebody to come along, pull us out, and guide us in a safer direction.

—Donald Miller

Meet Brooke

By the time Brooke had sought help for her eating disorder, she had limited her interactions with others to infrequent phone calls with her father and only necessary conversations with her coworkers. In an attempt to hide her eating disordered behaviors, and because of an increasing discomfort around food, she avoided situations where she would have to socialize with her family and friends. Now, as she is navigating the road to recovery, she is finding it difficult to reestablish her social network. She finds herself feeling unwanted, especially within her friend group, because they stopped inviting her to events after it became clear that she consistently declined their invitations. She is having difficulty creating distance from her family members, as she feels they have become overly involved with her life and well-being since her diagnosis. Brooke acknowledges the need to create a healthier support system but is unsure of where to start.

Individuals with anorexia tend to isolate from others for a variety of reasons. Like Brooke, you may have distanced yourself from your friends or family in an attempt to hide your eating disorder or to avoid situations involving food. Perhaps you avoided them because of anxiety or fear of judgment or because you were depressed and couldn't face the happy camaraderie of gatherings. Now that you are in recovery, developing a healthy social support network is an important—and often difficult—task. We will use the phrase "your social support network" broadly to include anyone who you interact with regularly or has an important role in your life: friends, family, professors, coworkers, employers, treatment team members, and significant others. Not only is having a strong and fulfilling social support system beneficial for your mental health and well-being, but creating a support system can also be beneficial by integrating your social network into your recovery.

Social Networks

Before proceeding with this chapter, let's take a moment to explore various components of a social network. Relationships with others involve varying degrees of intimacy, support, and reciprocity. Each level of intimacy or closeness affects your overall well-being and recovery. Within your inner circle are your relationships with high levels of support, intimacy, and reciprocity (close friends, family members, treatment team). Further out, you have your middle circle of support. These relationships demonstrate a moderate level of support, intimacy, and reciprocity (coworkers, classmates, less intense friendships). In your outer circle are relationships that demonstrate a low level of support, intimacy, and reciprocity (your boss, professors, acquaintances). The individuals who make up each circle will vary from person to person, so, as you continue through this chapter, keep this diagram in mind as you are examining where members of your support system currently fall and where you would like each of them to be.

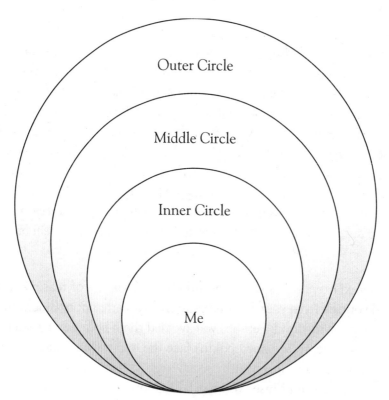

Healthy vs. Unhealthy Relationships

We often hear about relationships being healthy or unhealthy. But what makes a relationship *healthy* or *unhealthy*? One of the difficulties in using these terms is that relationships are typically not all one or the other. Instead, our relationships fall on a continuum of healthy to unhealthy, with a lot of gray area in between. For Brooke, her relationship with her parents has both healthy and unhealthy aspects: it is healthy because of their mutual love and respect, and it is unhealthy because their current concern for her well-being is limiting Brooke's independence. *Healthy* and *unhealthy* vary depending on several factors, including the nature of the relationship, the role someone plays in your life, your intimacy or closeness with that person, your personal needs and wants, and the other individual's needs and wants. A healthy relationship with your significant other looks very different from a healthy relationship with a parent, acquaintance, psychotherapist, boss, or professor.

Despite the variety of relationships we have, relationships that fall on the healthy side of the continuum likely have the following characteristics: mutual respect, dignity, open communication, honesty, and trust. Healthy relationships tend to foster personal growth and promote a balance between independence and dependence. Take some time to think about what it is that you want and need from your relationships. What are some attributes that relationships in your life must have for them to be healthy for you? Write your ideas in the space below. If you are having trouble, use your psychotherapist as a sounding board to help you explore and articulate what a healthy relationship means for you.

- _____
- _____
- _____
- _____
- _____

Similar to healthy relationships, what constitutes an *unhealthy* relationship often depends on the specifics of each relationship. However, there are some factors that are unhealthy in any relationship: any kind of abuse (verbal, physical, emotional, or sexual), excessive blaming by one or both parties, unwarranted or high levels of jealousy, repeated criticism and judgment, or coercion and controlling behavior. Now take some time to think about the attributes that the relationships in your life must *not* have? What constitutes an unhealthy relationship for you? Write your ideas on the next page. Again, if you are having difficulty, consult with your psychotherapist.

- _____
- _____
- _____
- _____
- _____

Now, let's apply this information to your current relationships. Just as Brooke did in the chart below, make a list of people in your life whom you have or would like to have in the inner or middle circles of your social support network (friends, parents, relatives, treatment team members, coworkers, peers) and those who might be in the outer circle of your support system (boss, professors, peers, coworkers). You may choose to list specific people (your mother or your best friend) and groups of people (peers in your classes or your extended family). Next, on a scale from 1 to 10 (1 being extremely unhealthy, and 10 being extremely healthy), rate how healthy you perceive your current relationship with each individual or group of individuals to be. Use the guidance provided above as a starting point to determine your ratings. In the final two columns, identify both the healthy and the unhealthy aspects of each relationship. Remember that most relationships have a mixture.

Relationship	Rating	Healthy Aspects	Unhealthy Aspects
Father	_5_	_He is supportive of my recovery._ _Mutual love and respect._ _We are working in family therapy together._	_I feel smothered by him._ _I blame him too much._ _I struggle to be independent from him._
Stepmother	_3_	_She is supportive of my recovery._	_Poor communication._ _She is very critical of me._ _I blame her a lot._
My friend group	_4_	_Mutual care and respect._	_I've isolated myself from them._ _I don't feel connected to them anymore._

Now complete the chart as it pertains to your relationships. This chart is also available at http://www.newharbinger.com/39348.

Relationship	Rating	Healthy Aspects	Unhealthy Aspects

Before moving on to the next section of this chapter, take some time to reflect on the work you have done so far. How are you feeling after identifying and analyzing your current relationships? What surprised you? Where did you have the most difficulty? What thoughts do you notice yourself having in response to the chart above?

_____

_____

_____

_____

Balancing Healthy and Unhealthy Aspects of Relationships

Building and maintaining your social network and support system is a balancing act of increasing the healthy aspects of the relationships in your life and decreasing the unhealthy ones. You identified and examined your current relationships in the prior section; now, let's discuss how to handle these relationships in ways that are conducive to your recovery. There are many ways one can approach this process, such as by setting and respecting boundaries, shifting roles, decreasing or increasing investment, and maintaining autonomy. Typically, a combination of several or all of these approaches is necessary to navigate your way to creating a network that is healthy *for you*.

Setting and Respecting Boundaries

Creating and maintaining boundaries is a difficult but necessary process for any relationship. When you realize a relationship is unhealthy or not meeting your needs, examining your boundaries in that relationship can help you gain insight into where changes need to be made. Boundaries are the explicit and implicit "rules" you have in a relationship; they can be openly stated (e.g., telling someone it is not okay to touch you sexually), or they can be implied (e.g., a societal understanding that it is not okay for particular people, such as professors, therapists, and parents, to touch you sexually). Boundaries can be physical, verbal, emotional, psychological, or sexual in nature, and they can be respected and upheld or violated. Setting and understanding these rules in relationships is complicated, as boundaries vary depending on the nature of the relationship, the role the other person plays in your life, your intimacy or closeness with that person, your personal needs and wants, and the other's needs and wants.

Below is a short list of healthy boundaries. Check off ones that you have been able to set.

_____ Saying no to others' requests

_____ Asking for help

_____ Accepting when others say no to you

_____ Treating yourself with respect

_____ Treating others with respect

_____ Maintaining your values despite what others think or say

_____ Staying focused on your recovery

_____ Noticing when someone displays inappropriate boundaries

_____ Clearly communicating your wants and needs to others

_____ Sharing personal information in appropriate ways (not over- or undersharing)

_____ Developing appropriate trust over time

_____ Evaluating whether a relationship is good for you

Because of the complexity of relationships, this process of setting and respecting healthy boundaries can be confusing and difficult. There are a variety of reasons boundaries are not always clearcut and simple, making them more likely to be crossed or violated.

Assumptions. As mentioned earlier, many of our boundaries are implicit—they are not stated aloud but are understood to exist because of general cultural, societal, or social expectations. For example, it is generally expected that others will remain outside your personal space unless you give permission, verbally or nonverbally, otherwise. Because many of our boundaries tend to be unspoken, it is easy to make assumptions when one is unsure of how to act, think, or feel with others. In fact, making assumptions is a completely normal response and a necessary skill. However, assumptions are not always accurate. For example, when Brooke's friends stopped asking her to spend time with them, she assumed that they no longer liked her. In recovery, as she began to reconnect with her friends, she realized that they still cared about her, they just stopped asking her to hang out because she always said no. If you notice a relationship or inter-action is unhealthy, uncomfortable, or causing a negative emotional response, take a step back and think about where you and the others involved may have made faulty assumptions. Usually, one assumption can lead to others making assumptions, so it is not as important to pinpoint who made the first inaccurate assumption. Instead, focus on the fact that incorrect assump-tions were made and use effective communication skills (described later in this chapter) to correct them.

Mind reading. Mind reading is similar to assumptions—we believe that we know what another person is thinking and feeling. We can also fall into the trap of expecting others to read our minds and know what we need or want (*My mother should know that talking about her diet in front of me is triggering!*). Many times, when our boundaries are not being respected, it is because we are expecting others to know what those boundaries are—but perhaps they don't understand them. If you catch yourself having thoughts that include the words *should know* with regard to the way someone else is behaving or reacting, take a step back and consider if explicitly telling this person of your needs and wants would be helpful.

Ineffective communication. Sometimes we do verbally inform others of our needs or boundaries, but the manner in which we do so is ineffective. Effective communication occurs when informa-tion is provided from one person and accurately received and interpreted by another person.

Common barriers to effective communication include being emotionally aroused, feeling overwhelmed or stressed, or not having your basic needs (e.g., food, safety, sleep) met, all of which can alter the other individual's interpretation or ability to receive your message. Effective communication skills, assertiveness skills, and interpersonal effectiveness will be discussed in detail later in this chapter. For now, if you notice that your boundaries are not being respected, take time to reflect on your communication style and consider if there are factors that may be inhibiting your ability to communicate effectively. Brooke struggled with communicating effectively because she was afraid to ask for what she wanted from others. Part of her treatment now focuses on challenging that fear and using skills to ask for what she wants.

Unrealistic expectations. Despite many efforts, there are times when even the most effective communicators are unable to get their needs met. One reason may be that we set unrealistic expectations for others. For example, you may need your best friend to be available to talk and support you several times per day, but your friend is feeling overwhelmed from trying to maintain your relationship while not neglecting other parts of her life. You can begin to manage this common pitfall by defining what roles you want others in your life to take and getting feedback regarding how realistic your expectations are. On the other hand, you may notice that others are setting unrealistic expectations for you. Instances like these require effective communication skills (which we will discuss later in this chapter). For now, take some time to consider which relationships in your life may be strained because of unrealistic expectations being set by you or others.

Interpersonal style. Finally, everyone has different ways of interacting and dealing with interpersonal issues. Similarly, the individuals involved in the relationship may have different goals, intentions, needs, and wants related to the relationship. Boundaries may be violated because of circumstances out of your control. We can only control our own behavior and interactions. Sometimes, despite our best efforts, our interpersonal styles are too incompatible with others'. In such cases, we may continue trying different ways of communicating our boundaries and needs, alter our expectations, or accept the limits of the other person and that relationship and seek to meet our needs in other ways.

BOUNDARIES QUIZ

Before moving on, take a moment to gauge your understanding of each of these common difficulties with establishing and maintaining boundaries. In the exercise below, label each of Brooke's statements as either an assumption, an example of mind reading, ineffective communication, an unrealistic expectation, or a difference in interpersonal style.

1. *My stepmother really should know that the constant criticism of my progress in recovery is only making it harder.*

   This is an example of _____.

2. Brooke wants to socialize with her coworkers in an effort to build better relationships with them. However, this is not congruent with the atmosphere of her workplace. Everyone typically keeps to themselves while at work.

   This is an example of _____.

3. *I want my friends to be there for me any time I'm struggling. I wish they would make an effort to eat meals with me throughout the week.*

   This is an example of _____.

4. *My dad just doesn't get it. He is so intrusive and smothering, and it just makes me want to avoid him even more than I already do. How does he not see that?*

   This is an example of _____.

5. Any time Brooke feels overwhelmed by her father's involvement in her treatment and life, she becomes irate and yells at him to leave her alone.

   This is an example of _____.

BOUNDARIES QUIZ ANSWERS

1. *My stepmother really should know that the constant criticism of my progress in recovery is only making it harder.*

   This is an example of mind reading. Brooke is expecting her stepmother to know how she feels and how her stepmother's comments affect her even though she has not talked with her about it before.

2. Brooke wants to socialize with her coworkers in an effort to build better relationships with them. However, this is not congruent with the atmosphere of her workplace. Everyone typically keeps to themselves while at work.

   This is an example of differences in interpersonal style. Brooke wants to foster better relationships in a setting that does not support such interactions.

3. *I want my friends to be there for me any time I'm struggling. I wish they would make an effort to eat meals with me throughout the week.*

   This is an example of unrealistic expectations. Brooke wants her friends to be highly attentive to her recovery needs, which is likely too much for her friends to handle. Also, because of her isolation from them, the expectation for them to suddenly be in tune with her needs is unrealistic.

4. *My dad just doesn't get it. He is so intrusive and smothering, and it just makes me want to avoid him even more than I already do. How does he not see that?*

   This is an example of making an assumption. Brooke is assuming that her father knows his behavior feels intrusive and smothering to her and that he understands why she is pushing away as a result of it.

5. Any time Brooke feels overwhelmed by her father's involvement in her treatment and life, she becomes irate and yells at him to leave her alone.

   This is an example of ineffective communication. Rather than explaining her feelings when she is in a calm state, Brooke is trying to address her needs in an angry state and without clear explanation of her emotions.

Shifting Roles

As mentioned earlier, the role others take or that you expect them to take in your life is an important aspect of a relationship. In order to increase healthy and positive relationships and decrease unhealthy and toxic relationships, shifting roles may be required. When you were in the throws of your eating disorder, others were likely to take on different roles than they had when you were healthy, partly in response to your ill state and partly in response to your changed interpersonal behavior (e.g., high irritability, isolation, anger outbursts) resulting from starvation or malnutrition. For example, Brooke's family took on a caretaker role when she was acutely ill, and now that she is in recovery, she is trying to navigate the shift back to a more parental or coadult role). Additionally, a relationship's level of intimacy can change. Brooke's relationship with her friends has waxed and waned in intimacy in terms of emotional support, social engagement, and reciprocity throughout her illness. She has also added new friends to her support network. Now that you are in recovery, it may be necessary for the roles and levels of intimacy with your family and friends to once again shift, just as Brooke has discovered. Some shifts may happen naturally. You may feel more energized and therefore are more likely to spend meaningful time with friends, or because you are not medically unstable, your parents may not take on as much of a caretaking role. Other shifts may require conscious effort.

To begin this process of shifting roles, you must first decide what you need and want from your social support network—for example, someone to provide you with accurate feedback, someone to have fun with, someone with whom you can be completely honest, or someone who helps you feel balanced. Do you need support during meals, emotional support, safety, monitoring of your weight, check-ins regarding intake, accountability, or someone to share successes with? Just as Brooke has done below, take some time to list these needs and wants. Consult with your psychotherapist to help you create a well-rounded list.

Brooke's Needs and Wants in Relationships

- *Validation and support in my recovery*

- *Social interaction*

- *A sense of acceptance and belonging*

- *A relationship not centered around my eating disorder*

- *Monitoring of my physical health*

Your Needs and Wants in Relationships

- _____

- _____

- _____

- _____

- _____

The items you have listed are going to serve as your "word bank" as you complete the following chart. In the first column, list the items from your word bank. In the second column, write down who currently fulfills each need or role in your life and rate them on a scale of 1 to 10 on how effective they are at meeting your needs (higher numbers indicating more effective). In the third column, list those who you want to fulfill these roles and needs. Remember that more than one individual or group of people can meet the same needs. Finally, in the fourth column, reflect on what would need to change for you to feel that each role or need you listed is fulfilled. See Brooke's example before trying the exercise on your own. This exercise is also available at http://www.newharbinger.com/39348.

What roles do I need others to fill in my life?	Who currently fulfills this role? How well?	Whom do I want to fulfill this role?	What would need to change for me to feel that this role is fulfilled?
Validation and support in my recovery	_My therapist (9)_ _My father (4)_ _Stepmother (2)_	_My therapist, my family, my friends_	_Attending all my appointments, connecting to friends better, more family therapy_
A sense of acceptance and belonging	_Friends (4)_ _Coworkers (7)_ _Family (5)_	_My family, friends, coworkers, classmates_	_Being authentic and vulnerable in my relationships_
Monitoring of my physical health	_Treatment team (10)_ _My father (2)_	_Only my treatment team_	_Setting boundaries with my father about not being intrusive in monitoring my health_

What roles do I need others to fill in my life?	Who currently fulfills this role? How well?	Whom do I want to fulfill this role?	What would need to change for me to feel that this role is fulfilled?

Before moving on, take some time to process what came up for you in the space below. These questions can help guide your reflection: What relationships have the largest discrepancies? How do you feel after completing this exercise? What have you learned about yourself (such as your needs in relationships and your expectations of others) through this exercise? It might be worthwhile to also discuss your reflections with your psychotherapist.

_____

_____

_____

_____

Decreasing and Increasing Investment

Sometimes shifting roles does not work, perhaps because certain people in your life cannot meet your needs and expectations or maybe they are not willing to make such a shift. Either way, it is necessary at times to practice acceptance and manage relationships in a different way. Acceptance does not mean that you give up or allow unhealthy or harmful relationships to continue to negatively influence your recovery and life. Instead, part of acceptance is accepting that you have to take another route, such as decreasing investment in such relationships.

You may choose to decrease the amount of time you spend with someone or to put restrictions on how you interact with him or her. For example, if you have a friend who is continuously dieting, you may choose to not spend mealtimes with her. You may also choose to decrease the amount of emotional investment you put into a particular relationship. For example, you may need to devalue toxic relationships by not allowing them to carry as much importance in your life. This is a less tangible change than the strategy described above. Instead, it is more of an internal change in perception and a putting of your values first. Additionally, there may be relationships in your life that are important to you and that you don't want to lose, but these individuals may not be providing you with the type of support and understanding you need at this point in time. It may be difficult to do, but you may need to modify your expectations of people and relationships to help reduce your risk of being hurt, disappointed, or having your recovery process undermined.

While decreasing unhealthy relationships is sometimes essential, it is often hard to do so, as you may think *I would rather have these relationships than none at all*, *These are the only relationships I have; I can't decrease my investment in them without feeling lonely*, or *These are the only people who would want to be my friends. Who else would care about me?* These are likely experiences, particularly for individuals with anorexia, as your eating disorder may have caused conflict in, loss of interest in, or withdrawal from your relationships. It may also cause you to devalue yourself, leading you to put up with negative or unhealthy relationships and being treated poorly by others. For these reasons, increasing investment in healthy and positive relationships is arguably more important than decreasing your investment in the negative ones. The more healthy relationships we have in our lives, the less we need to hold on to the unhealthy ones.

Before continuing, there are two important points to consider. First, engaging in positive relationships and creating meaningful connections with others may be complicated by factors other than your eating disorder, such as anxiety or depression. It may be necessary for you to address these issues with your psychotherapist prior to or during this process of investing in new and healthy relationships. Second, as you increase your investment in healthy relationships, it is important to balance quantity and quality. Both are necessary; however, we do not want to compromise one for the other. It is important to have multiple meaningful people in our networks.

The first step, and possibly the hardest step, for engaging in meaningful, healthy relationships is putting yourself out there and being vulnerable. This requires both external and internal work. The external work may include joining a support group, volunteering, participating in clubs and sports, or browsing the Internet for special-interest organizations and groups in your community in which you can meet others with similar interests. External work may also involve consciously using the interpersonal skills described later in this chapter and using committed action (discussed in chapter 6) to motivate yourself to interact with others and to overcome fears or anxieties about rejection. You may need to initiate plans with friends or ask what others are doing for fun. Internal work, on the other hand, includes discovering your passions and connecting with your values (discussed in chapter 6), which can guide you to develop relationships that are meaningful and fit with your aspirations in life. It also includes accepting your imperfections and being compassionate toward yourself when you make mistakes or experience self-doubt. It is also the work of staying motivated, picking yourself back up after a perceived rejection or negative interaction, and continuing to practice establishing, maintaining, and engaging in new and healthy relationships. By working through the internal distress and discomfort and putting yourself in situations that give you the opportunity to have new and positive experiences and interactions with others, you eventually can prove to yourself that you are capable and worthy of meaningful connections with others.

Before moving on, take a minute to reflect on relationships. Are there some for which you need to decrease your investment? How are these relationships unhealthy for you? What barriers might you face in decreasing your investment in those relationships?

_____

_____

_____

Are there relationships in which you would like to increase your investment? What are some external actions you can take to increase your investment in relationships? What internal work do you need to do?

_____

_____

_____

Maintaining Autonomy

Much of what has been covered so far in this chapter focuses on being part of a social network and appropriately utilizing others for support. However, it is important to remember that maintaining autonomy and a sense of self is also necessary. *Autonomy* means being able to rely on yourself and feeling able to deal with challenges and experience joys independently and concurrently with others.

Fostering autonomy starts with sitting with yourself and learning to tolerate, and eventually enjoy, your own company. You may try challenging yourself by doing an activity alone, such as walking mindfully, eating dinner at a restaurant, or journaling at a coffee shop. While it is easy to engage in activities that require significant effort and attention on the task at hand, it is more difficult, but also more rewarding, to develop the skills to participate in activities where you can observe and accept your thoughts and feelings rather than avoid them.

Make a list of activities that you can engage in that foster your sense of autonomy.

- _____
- _____
- _____
- _____
- _____

Interpersonal Skills

In the last section, we covered several approaches to dealing with relationships in your life: setting boundaries, shifting the roles in your relationships, and decreasing or increasing investment in relationships, as well as maintaining autonomy. In order to put those techniques into action, you may need to develop or improve your interpersonal skills. Your eating disorder may have often left you isolated and involved in unhealthy relationships, and that can decrease your ability to effectively interact with others in a way that fosters healthy relationships and satisfies your emotional, physical, and psychological needs. Just as with any other skill, interpersonal skills require practice. Below are some skills that are required to build and manage healthy relationships. As we discuss them, take some time to reflect on how you utilize each of these in your life.

Self-Awareness

One of the most important interpersonal skills you can develop has very little to do with others. Being *self-aware*—observing your thoughts, feelings, and actions from an objective point of view—is important for establishing healthy relationships. While you are interacting with others, you may ask yourself the following questions to help your self-awareness:

- What am I feeling? Thinking? Doing?

- Am I reacting (being defensive, irritable, or judgmental) or responding (taking time to think about the situation)?

- Am I being a people pleaser (not taking into consideration my own needs or boundaries)?

- Am I overstepping (not respecting others' boundaries or not taking their needs into consideration)?

- How are my interactions in this moment affecting or going to affect my relationships with others?

Another area of self-awareness you may want to consider is your authenticity. Being aware of your authenticity can give you insight as to why your connections with others may not be as meaningful or intimate as you need and want. Brené Brown has written extensively about authenticity and its role in harboring a sense of belonging and connectedness with others: "Fitting in is about assessing a situation and becoming who you need to be to be accepted. Belonging, on the other hand, doesn't require us to change who we are; it requires us to be who we are... Because true belonging only happens when we present our authentic, imperfect selves to the world, our sense of belonging can never be greater than our level of self-acceptance" (2010, 25–26).

So ask yourself: Are you being authentic—true to yourself—and presenting that version of yourself to others? How can you improve upon this in your relationships?

_____

_____

_____

_____

_____

Effective Communication

Communication skills may seem commonsense, but we often slip into ineffective means of communicating when we are emotional, stressed, tired, or simply unaware of our style of interacting. We will go through three noteworthy techniques for effective communication that you can review, practice, and implement: direct communication, taking breaks, and using "I-statements." You can also discuss these with your psychotherapist.

Direct communication. This, simply enough, means being assertive and telling others in clear terms what you feel or think. We are not mind readers, and we cannot always expect others to know what we need or want. Common hindrances to using direct communication include anxiety about potentially upsetting the other person, relying too heavily on nonverbal communication, assuming others know or remember what your needs are, and feeling that your needs are not important or you are not deserving of having a voice. Challenge yourself to explicitly say what you need and want from others, and remember that you may have to repeat yourself for others to understand. Work with your psychotherapist to overcome barriers that may be getting in the way of your ability to make statements such as "What I need from you is…" and "When I'm upset, I would like for you to…"

Take a moment to think about a couple of situations in which you can practice direct communication. Write down whom you are talking with and what you want to clearly communicate, and consider any barriers that get in your way of communicating directly. See Brooke's example below to get you started.

Brooke: *My dad is supportive of my recovery, but he gets overbearing at times, asking me too many questions. I know he means well, but I want him to stop asking me how I'm doing all the time. I would like to clearly communicate that I need him to have faith in me and my treatment team and that I will alert him if I'm not doing well in recovery. What would get in my way of being successful is that I don't want to hurt my dad's feelings, because I know he is asking me because he cares about my well-being.*

Now you try:

1. _____

_____

_____

2. _____

_____

_____

3. _____

_____

_____

Taking a break. When you are emotionally aroused, simply taking a break can help you communicate effectively. We are more likely to be accusatory, raise our voices, shut down, storm out of a room, and say things we do not mean when we are in an emotional, aroused state. While the emotions you're feeling may be entirely appropriate for the situation, they are not the most helpful ways to get others to hear us. Taking a break can help you get back to your emotional baseline. This will allow you to think more rationally and clearly, which, in turn, will help you communicate more directly. Remember that taking a break is effective only if you return to the issue or conversation at hand! Also, taking a break without a warning to the other person can escalate an issue, because he or she may interpret it as you being disrespectful or immature. It may be beneficial to tell your friends and family ahead of time that you may need to take breaks from emotionally triggering conversations and explain why. Or you can create and practice using a brief statement that you can say in the moment to let others know what you are doing. For example, you may say, "I'm sorry, but I need to take a break. After I calm down, I'll be better able to talk with you."

Consider past times when it would have been helpful for you to take a break because you were emotionally charged during a conversation. With whom were you talking? What emotion were you feeling? What got in the way of you taking a break from the conversation? What could you have said that would have allowed you to step away briefly before returning to the conversation once your emotions had decreased?

_____

_____

_____

_____

_____

I-statements. I-statements are an effective way of communicating your feelings with others in a way that is not threatening to them. These statements put the focus on how you feel rather than what the other person may have done wrong, which helps others not feel blamed for their actions or get defensive. It allows an opportunity for a conversation to happen. For example, the following statements may seem like they say the same thing, but the underlying messages are different: "You make me so anxious because you talk about my body so much," versus "I feel really anxious when you talk about my body, because it reminds me of how uncomfortable I feel at this weight." The first statement places blame on the other person and is likely to evoke a defensive response or reciprocate blame ("I'm just give you a compliment!" or "Well, if you would just gain weight, I wouldn't have to talk about how thin you look."). The second version, the I-statement, is less likely to provoke such a response, because the focus is about you and your feelings rather than the other person's actions. Remember that others cannot *make* us feel anything. Our feelings arise from our evaluation of the event, not the event itself. That is why someone making comments about another person's weight may evoke anxiety in one person, while in others it may bring up feelings of sadness, anger, fear, indifference, satisfaction, or excitement. The next time you are trying to communicate your feelings, try putting your thoughts into the following formula to help you convey your feelings effectively: *I feel _____ when _____ because _____.*

Practice writing out some ideas before speaking to help them feel more natural. Brooke completed one for you to follow.

Brooke: I feel *hurt* when *I'm not invited to hang out with you* because *I feel left out and would like to try to reconnect with you.*

I feel _____ when _____

_____

because _____.

I feel _____ when _____

_____

because _____.

Expressing Appreciation

When others respond to our efforts the way we want, it is easy to take it for granted. Take time to acknowledge when others say or do things that help your recovery. Thanking your supports and letting them know that how they are responding to or interacting with you is helpful and beneficial to you can reinforce their actions and build stronger and more satisfying relationships. A small thank-you or action demonstrating appreciation can help you to maintain relationships and communicate effectively with others. The next time someone supports you in a positive manner, try expressing your appreciation using the following formula to help you convey your feelings effectively: *I want to thank you for _____ when _____ because _____.*

Practice writing out some ideas before speaking them to help them feel more natural. See Brooke's example on the next page.

Brooke: I want to thank you for *inviting me* when *you went to the movies last week* because *it meant a lot to me to be included, even though I couldn't make it.*

I want to thank you for _____ when _____

_____

because _____.

I want to thank you for _____ when _____

_____

because _____.

Taking a New Perspective

It is important to put yourself in others' shoes to try and understand where they are coming from. By taking a step back and hypothesizing about why others may have said or done something you did not like, you can think about situations more objectively. When we take the time to understand what has led someone to behave in a certain way, we avoid jumping to conclusions based on our own reactions. We are more likely to take things personally or attribute negative qualities to someone when we feel hurt, angry, or insulted. This is common and understandable. Allow yourself to feel hurt; your feelings are valid. But then challenge yourself to also think about events from the other person's perspective. Doing so helps us build empathy and maintain relationships.

Think about a situation in which you might have benefited from looking at it from someone else's perspective. Take a minute to jot down your thoughts about your perspective in that situation, what the other person's perspective might have been, and how it would have been helpful for you to consider the other person's perspective at the time.

_____

_____

Teamwork

Finally, try viewing your support network as a team. You are all working together for a common goal: recovery from your eating disorder. It can surely feel as if others in your life are angry with you or fighting against you, but they are actually fighting against your eating disorder. Take accountability for your slips, overreactions, or disordered behaviors without externalizing blame onto other people or situations. Doing so may help alleviate some of the defensiveness you find yourself succumbing to when you feel like others are against you. Keep your social network informed of your needs, your struggles, your successes, and your progress. Let them in as much as you feel is appropriate, and accept support when it is offered. You do not have to fight your eating disorder alone!

Who would you consider part of your team? _____

_____

Is there anything that you need to hold yourself accountable for?

_____

How can you approach your team to get support from them?

_____

Journaling Pages

In this chapter, we discussed the following topics: isolation, healthy and unhealthy relationships, setting and maintaining boundaries, shifting roles as you move forward in recovery, altering investment in relationships, maintaining autonomy, and interpersonal skills (self-awareness, effective communication, taking other's perspectives, expressing appreciation, and teamwork). We offered many exercises to practice and reflect on these concepts. Take some time to reflect on your patterns of thinking, feeling, and behaving in relationships. Are there specific relationships for which boundaries are harder to set or respect than others? When and in what ways do you find yourself falling into the pitfalls in maintaining boundaries described above (making assumptions, mind reading, ineffective communication, unrealistic expectations, and faulty interpersonal style)? What are some skills you can use to work on creating healthier relationships? We encourage you to review your thoughts with your psychotherapist.

Chapter 11

Engaging in Self-Care

Self-care is never a selfish act—it is simply good stewardship of the only gift I have, the gift I was put on earth to offer others. Anytime we can listen to true self and give the care it requires, we do it not only for ourselves, but for the many others whose lives we touch.

—Parker Palmer

Meet Ashley

Ashley has been working actively and consistently on her recovery, but she has been feeling quite overwhelmed with it all. With three appointments with various treatment team members, a group therapy session, two classes for school, and a part-time job to juggle each week, she is struggling to find time to relax and to find enjoyment in her life. When she does successfully integrate some downtime into her week, she experiences significant guilt because she does not perceive it as productive. She also fears that her feelings of being overwhelmed will only increase if she schedules more into her days. Feeling stuck, she has decided to bring this up in her next psychotherapy session.

In a society that glorifies being busy and productive, it is easy to devalue leisure and self-care activities. Especially as you begin working on your recovery, taking time to do fun or relaxing things can feel indulgent, selfish, and wrong. Like Ashley, you can feel guilty about taking time off, or you may feel overwhelmed by adding to all that you already have to do. However, engaging in activities that you enjoy and find fulfilling is a relevant part of recovery and life in general. Engaging in self-care creates a balance in your recovery, which often feels like a never-ending, exhausting, and painful process. Experiencing joy and pleasure is part of what makes recovery feel worth it, and it makes life meaningful.

What Is Self-Care?

Self-care is the process of intentionally engaging in activities that promote all aspects of your well-being—your physical, psychological, emotional, spiritual, professional or academic, interpersonal, and personal well-being. Self-care activities are best experienced when they are balanced and healthy. This means focusing on each of the aspects of your well-being and ensuring that you are engaging in activities that enrich your life in each one; it is also important that you do not focus on any one aspect at the expense of another. Ashley seems to be struggling with this concept of a healthy balance. She is taking care of her psychological and physical self by attending her appointments with her various treatment providers, and she is tending to her professional and academic life through school and work. However, she is having difficulty attending to her personal and emotional well-being, resulting in increased levels of stress. Balance is an important part of self-care, especially when recovering from an eating disorder. It is important that your focus on self-care not become another burden or pressure in your life. Self-care is meant to be helpful to you. The goal is not to strive for a perfect balance in all aspects of your life or to rigidly follow your list of self-care activities each day. It is best to have a flexible approach to self-care and balance, seeing yourself as a work in progress, slowly trying to get better at self-care over time. You should make a reasonable effort to strive for balance in your life, knowing that it will never be perfect and that it is the ongoing effort, not the results achieved, that matters most.

Self-Care Questionnaire

Before we begin identifying ways for you to improve your self-care practices, take a moment to assess your current self-care activities. The list below is not a to-do list, but rather a list of potential ways to practice self-care. The expectation is not for you to engage in 100 percent of these items on a daily basis, and this list is by no means exhaustive. Use this list as a starting point for evaluating your self-care practices and needs. Rate each item in terms of how often you engage in each activity using a scale of 0 to 3: 0 (never), 1 (sometimes), 2 (often), or 3 (almost always).

Physical Well-Being

_____ I am maintaining a healthy weight.

_____ I exercise as recommended by my treatment team.

_____ I eat according to the recommendations of my treatment team.

_____ I get enough sleep.

_____ I take my medications as prescribed.

Psychological Well-Being

____ I attend my scheduled appointments with my various treatment team members.

____ I practice what I have learned in therapy in my daily life.

____ I go to support groups that help my recovery.

____ I take time to practice self-reflection.

____ I strive for balance in my daily life.

Emotional Well-Being

____ I take time to participate in relaxing activities.

____ I take time to engage in activities that I enjoy.

____ I use coping skills (such as journaling or listening to music) when needed.

____ I allow myself to feel a wide range of emotions.

Religious or Spiritual Well-Being

____ I attend to my religious or spiritual practices.

____ I engage in activities that bring me closer to my religious or spiritual side (praying, spending time in nature, or attending religious services).

Professional or Academic Well-Being

____ I take regularly scheduled breaks.

____ I set limits in terms of my workload and hours I work per week.

____ I say no to additional work when I feel overwhelmed by school or work.

____ I keep up with my work or schoolwork and meet deadlines.

Interpersonal Well-Being

_____ I have a support network that I can and do rely on.

_____ I make an effort to spend quality time with my friends.

_____ I make an effort to spend quality time with my family.

_____ I socialize outside of work or school.

_____ I spend time with my significant other.

Personal Well-Being

_____ I take vacations periodically.

_____ I have interests and hobbies that I attend to regularly.

_____ I create and follow a budget.

_____ I take care of my household chores in a timely manner.

_____ I maintain my hygiene.

Beginning with the Basics

Having gathered some baseline information for yourself, the next step is to brainstorm self-care activities that you want to integrate into your life. These can include things from the list above; however, it is also important to develop a repertoire of self-care strategies that are specific and relevant to you. It's best to begin with the basics of self-care, including your essential needs, such as sleep, food, safety, and medications. Without these needs being met, it is difficult to reap the benefits of—or engage meaningfully in—other self-care activities that focus on relationships, leisure, and growth. Psychologist Abraham Maslow represents this idea well with his concept of a hierarchy of needs (1943). Maslow asserts that our needs must be met in the following order: physiological, safety and security, love and belonging, esteem, and self-actualization, as illustrated in the figure opposite.

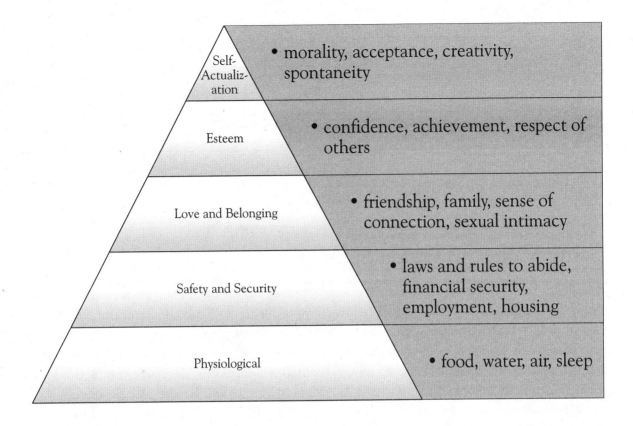

According to Maslow, our most basic needs (food, water, air, sleep, safety, security) must be met before we can focus energy on and find meaningful our psychological needs (love, belonging, and esteem) and self-actualization needs (expressing creativity, contributing to society, the pursuit of knowledge, the desire for self-growth).

The tricky thing about recovery from an eating disorder is that you do, in fact, need to meet your basic needs first, but you need to work on your higher-level needs at the same time, as recovery from an eating disorder is not as simple as "just eating." It may feel like a catch-22: you need to eat, drink, and be physically well before you can find meaning in things like intimacy, connection, and self-confidence, *and* you need to find meaning in life and within yourself to feel worthy of, capable of, and motivated for keeping yourself physically well. This is a dialectic that we must continue to monitor and balance. Therefore, it is important for us to take some time to establish your basic self-care needs *and* identify and work on increasing higher-level self-care activities that can fulfill your sense of love, belonging, esteem, and self-actualization.

Focusing on your basic needs (physiological, plus safety and security), on the next page create a list of ways you can practice self-care. Some ideas may include going to bed at the same time every night, going to bed earlier, taking your medication as prescribed, and following your meal plan. Include things you are already doing and ways in which you would like to add to or improve your basic self-care.

1. _____

2. _____

3. _____

4. _____

5. _____

Using Values to Guide Self-Care

While you may not be able to meet all of your basic needs all the time, you can still strive to incorporate self-care activities associated with your higher-level needs (love and belonging, esteem, and self-actualization). One way to find self-care strategies that are meaningful and helpful to you is to look to your values for guidance. In chapter 6, you identified your core values, and throughout this book we have referenced them as a compass to help guide your actions and decisions. Refresh your memory on what your values are, as we will be using them once again.

When we use our values as guides for changes in behavior, we are more likely to find the changes to be meaningful, fulfilling, and important to our overall well-being. Similarly, if we create self-care strategies that help us feel more connected to our values, we are more likely to find them worthwhile and continue doing them. Thinking about each value as an overarching category, what are ways that you can enhance or improve each value in your life?

Using Ashley's example below for guidance, complete the following activity by labeling each "values box" with one of your values and then listing examples of self-care that you would enjoy or would be willing to try. One self-care activity can be related to more than one value, but it would be best to list it only under one so that you can add as many activities as possible. Use the following questions to guide your reflections as you take time to think about each value: How do I currently make efforts to connect to this value? What do I wish I could do to live closer in line with this value? In what environments can I find this value in my life? This exercise is also available at http://www.newharbinger.com/39348.

Ashley's Values Boxes

Learning/Knowledge

Take classes I enjoy

Attend my classes

Choose a major

Read for fun

Beauty

Take pictures

Spend time outside

Go to art museums

Visit a national park

Friendship

Spend time with friends

Host a party

Initiate plans

Go to events I'm invited to

Inner Peace

Do yoga

Meditate

Do deep breathing exercises

Go to therapy to work through my trauma

Your Values Boxes

Daily Self-Care Activities

There may be additional self-care strategies that do not fit neatly into any of your values boxes or that are small and subtle day-to-day acts that we often forget. These can still be helpful to you, as your values are merely a representation of what is important to you; your values boxes don't represent an exhaustive list of what you value. Using the sample list below as suggestions, create another list of self-care strategies that focuses on items that may not have been captured in your values boxes. Remember that this is not a list of things you need to do every day, but rather a list of self-care strategies we can select from and practice on an ongoing basis.

Examples of Day-to-Day Self-Care Strategies

- Taking a bubble bath
- Playing with pets
- Spending quality time with friends or family
- Spending time outside
- Spending your lunch break outside (rather than at a desk)
- Taking deep breaths
- Staying organized
- Tending to hygiene and physical appearance
- Saying no when needed
- Laughing
- Attending religious or spiritual services and meetings
- Creating and following a budget
- Giving yourself a break
- Treating yourself to something nice
- Taking a walk
- Singing
- Taking a nap

Your Day-to-Day Self-Care Plan

Using the examples above as guidance, take a moment to think about ways you can take care of yourself on a daily basis. What types of day-to-day activities would you like to work on in order to improve your sense of well-being? List your top five ideas below.

1. _____

2. _____

3. _____

4. _____

5. _____

Your Self-Care Activities

So far, we have talked about self-care that meets your basic needs (food, water, sleep, shelter, medical stability, safety), self-care that is guided by your values, and self-care that can improve your day-to-day life. Let's take some time to put all of your ideas for self-care activities in one place. Using the chart on the next page to help you organize your ideas, list as many activities as you can that you feel will improve your sense of well-being and vitality. You can return to this chart at any time in your recovery to get an idea for self-care, to check in with yourself on how you are doing with keeping up with your self-care, and to add to it. This chart is also available at http://www.newharbinger.com/39348, so you can update it as you progress through recovery. Ashley provided one example for each section to get you started.

	Activities I Can Do Alone	Activities I Can Do With Others
Self-Care That Meets My Basic Needs	*Go to bed by eleven each night.*	*Go to dinner at my parents.*
Small Self-Care Activities That I Can Do in My Daily Life	*Sing on my drive to work.*	*Set healthy boundaries.*
More Time-Consuming Self-Care Activities	*Paint my nails.*	*Take a dance class.*

	Activities I Can Do Alone	Activities I Can Do With Others
Self-Care That Meets My Basic Needs		
Small Self-Care Activities That I Can Do in My Daily Life		
More Time-Consuming Self-Care Activities		

Integrating Self-Care into Recovery

Recovery is a simultaneous process of fighting or changing the negative (disordered thought patterns, eating behaviors, and body image) and rediscovering or enhancing the positive (fun, leisure, and social activities that make life worth living). It is important that you integrate the activities listed above into your life and find ways to balance all aspects of your recovery. However, creating time and putting effort into engaging in these activities is easier said than done. Many things get in the way of self-care, including busy schedules, unrealistic expectations, anxiety about trying new things, and guilt for engaging in such activities.

As noted, recovery from an eating disorder is time consuming! You are likely trying to integrate back into or keep up with your day-to-day schedule, and you probably have appointments with your treatment team throughout the week. Doing everyday activities differently (shopping for groceries, cooking, sitting with your emotions, resisting urges to act on disordered behaviors) also takes time and energy—and can be draining. The best way to integrate self-care into a busy week, particularly the larger or more time-consuming activities, is to schedule them. This may mean that you plan to dedicate an hour a week to playing an instrument or that you commit to going to bed at the same time each night. As for small, day-to-day self-care strategies, such as setting boundaries, eating snacks, or taking deep breaths, create reminders for yourself. You can put notes in places you will see them or set reminders on your smartphone. Regardless of the types of activities you begin to integrate into your life, start small and give yourself a chance to adjust to these changes in your daily routine. It may also be helpful to refer back to chapter 6 to help you create SMART and value-based goals for this process.

Putting Your Plan into Action

Having all of these ideas is a great start. In order to put them into action, you must create time and space to practice these strategies. Everyone has different methods for organizing, planning, scheduling, and getting motivated to implement change. Keeping in mind your individual style, complete the following sections to summarize ways you can add self-care to your life.

Some people use planners, calendars, alarms, or reminder notes. What are the most effective ways you can plan for and remind yourself of self-care activities?

_____

_____

_____

Thinking about your current routine, what are the best days and times for self-care activities?

_____

_____

_____

Sometimes you may need a reminder of why these activities are important to your recovery, especially when you're feeling too busy or overwhelmed to take care of yourself. What are the reasons and values you have for practicing self-care?

_____

_____

_____

_____

_____

Common Pitfalls

Engaging in self-care may seem straightforward, but if you are not aware of potential pitfalls, self-care activities may cause problems.

Self-Care vs. Perpetuating Your Eating Disorder

You may find yourself being motivated by your eating disorder to participate in self-care activities rather than by a desire to improve your life. For example, Ashley enjoys exercising. Physical activity is a common self-care activity in our society, and it may be enticing for her to begin an exercise routine. She knows that regular exercise improves her mood, and she therefore thinks that it would be an important activity to do for self-care. However, this will likely conflict with her treatment team's recommendations for her recovery, as overexercising is something she struggled with throughout her eating disorder. Also, Ashley's motivations for exercising may include burning calories or changing her body's shape rather than simply improving her physical health or social interactions. Ashley would need to be self-aware in evaluating if exercise is a good choice for a self-care activity. Likewise, it is important that you are self-aware, open with yourself and your treatment team regarding your motivations, and receptive to collaborating with your team to choose self-care activities that best fit your individual needs.

Self-Care as Avoidance

Another common pitfall is using a self-care activity as an avoidance strategy. This may take various forms. For example, you may find creating art extremely soothing for your problems with anxiety, and so you stay in on weekends to paint or create collages rather than socializing, since fear of not fitting in increases your social anxiety. This is not to say that creating art is always an avoidance tactic or that overcoming social fears and anxiety is as simple as forcing yourself to socialize on weekends. Instead, it is an example of behaviors that can lead to a cycle that furthers your isolation or anxiety in the long run, which defeats the purpose of self-care. Remember that self-care improves an aspect of your well-being without worsening another. Another way self-care may be used as avoidance is by doing too much of it. It is possible to fall into the pattern of over-scheduling yourself with self-care activities so that you begin to not have time to eat, go grocery shopping, or get sufficient sleep. Thus, we must maintain or promote balance in our lives, and self-care must be a part of that balance. To help you gauge how balanced your schedule and self-care routine are, think about your motivations, reflect on what you may be avoiding, look at other areas of your life (e.g., physical needs and health) to see if they are being tended to, and consult with your treatment team for an objective perspective.

Feeling Guilty or Selfish

As was described in Ashley's profile at the beginning of the chapter, feelings of guilt and viewing oneself as selfish or overly indulgent are common experiences when practicing self-care. However, self-care is not an indulgence, nor is it something you do only when you have time or as a reward for hard work. Instead, self-care is an ongoing necessity and an important component to your recovery and overall well-being. If you find yourself experiencing guilt as you venture on this journey of self-care, be open and honest about it both with yourself and your team. It is important to explore and work through the underlying factors contributing to your discomfort with practicing self-care in psychotherapy, as feelings of guilt, selfishness, and indulgence will only serve to inhibit your recovery process.

Getting Caught in Perfectionism and Comparisons

Finally, there is no perfect way to practice self-care. You are a unique person, and while many people in recovery from anorexia share similar struggles, your recovery journey is specific to you. The quantity and types of self-care activities that help you to function optimally are likely to be different from those for other individuals. No self-care activities are better than others, and there is no special list of self-care strategies you "should" be integrating into your life. Check in with yourself periodically. Are you comparing your self-care activities to how others practice self-care? Are you feeling inferior or superior to others because of your self-care routine? Are you feeling guilty if you do or do not engage in self-care activities? Do you overdo self-care at the expense of maintaining a healthy balance in your life? Take time in psychotherapy to process these perfectionistic tendencies if they arise. It is also important to remember that self-care is a skill we need to practice, to work at, and to develop comfort and proficiency with. It also is not all or nothing. We can start slowly and then, over time, build our self-care activities, slowly adding to them as we adapt and adjust to them. Trying to do too much or trying to achieve the "perfect" balance can be potential self-care pitfall.

My Potential Pitfalls

Self-awareness is important in recovery, particularly at times when your eating disorder has the potential to sneak into your thoughts and actions. Self-care can become an excuse to act on eating disordered behaviors, such as overexercising, restricting, or isolating. Obtain input from your treatment team and others who know you well, reflect on your own vulnerabilities, and complete the following sections to summarize ways you may slip into disordered thinking or behaviors.

There will likely be struggles as you begin to practice self-care. What things do you anticipate being particularly challenging?

_____

_____

_____

It will be important for you to know the warning signs that you're struggling to implement self-care into your life in a balanced and healthy manner. What are some things that may signal you're struggling?

_____

_____

_____

There will be times when you feel overwhelmed or burdened by your schedule. It will be tempting to reduce the amount of self-care you practice in order to make more time for other needs and responsibilities. When you're struggling to manage, you have many options: you can talk with others; you can ask for your treatment team's opinion as to what is reasonable to reduce or cut out; you can rely on others to keep you accountable; you can remind yourself that you need self-care in order to make recovery feel worthwhile and to have a clear mind to continue the difficult aspects of recovery. What will be most effective for you when you're feeling overwhelmed?

_____

_____

_____

If you notice you're struggling to manage your self-care routine, early intervention is key. You can lean on others and be honest with your treatment team, and you will need others to react in a way that is helpful to you. Which individuals can you lean on, and how can they respond when you're struggling?

For Support, You Can Contact...	He or She Can Help You By...

Sharing Your Self-Care Plan

When making positive changes for yourself and your recovery, it can be helpful to share your self-care plan with others. You might find it useful for your treatment team members, parents, or close friends to know your plan so they can help you manage your time and maintain balance, and they can check in with you on your progress as you integrate self-care strategies into your daily life. Just as you need others to keep you accountable for your disordered behaviors and thoughts, you could also benefit from using your supports to keep you accountable for self-care. Sharing this information with your loved ones can also help them understand your recovery in a more holistic way, rather than simply as "getting rid of your eating disorder." Complete the following exercise to identify the people you want involved in your self-care journey, and include details regarding how each person can help you in this process. This chart is also available at http://www.newharbinger .com/39348.

People I Want Involved	How They Can Best Help Me

Journaling Pages

In this chapter, we discussed self-care as it pertains to your life, recovery, and overall well-being. We differentiated between self-care that meets your basic needs, self-care that is driven by your values, and the day-to-day kinds of self-care that can further enrich your life. We also covered potential challenges and pitfalls you may encounter as you integrate self-care into your recovery. As you reflect on this chapter, how have your views of self-care changed? What are your thoughts about incorporating self-care into your recovery plan? What do you think will get in the way of recovery, and how can you overcome these barriers? What are some ways of practicing self-care that you have found work for you, and what are some ways you've discovered don't work for you? What are some self-care lessons you can take with you moving forward?

_____

_____

_____

_____

_____

_____

_____

_____

_____

_____

_____

_____

_____

Chapter 12

Managing and Preventing Relapses

[W]e may encounter many defeats, but we must not be defeated. It may even be necessary to encounter the defeat, so that we can know who we are... And that then that's how you get to know yourself. [...] That's how you get to know who you are.

—Maya Angelou

Meet Kiera

Kiera has been doing well in her recovery for several months now. However, in the past two years she experienced several significant relapses, each of which she perceives to have happened almost overnight. As a result, she is having a hard time trusting the process of recovery, as she feels like any progress she makes could be lost to a relapse at any moment. She tends to be triggered easily by her social circle, as many of her friends are into "clean eating" and tracking their fitness and diet goals. Thus, each time she has returned home from being hospitalized for her anorexia, she found herself immersed back in this culture of being intensely focused on diet and exercise and found it hard to be focused on her recovery, which includes eating a variety of foods, challenging herself to eat more fear foods, and exercising minimally until she is in a more solid place in her recovery. She experiences significant shame because of her relapses and is often harsh and critical toward herself when she has an urge or acts on an eating disordered behavior, which tends to perpetuate her behaviors rather than curb them. Unsure about how to manage such slips, Kiera finds herself feeling hopeless about maintaining her recovery.

Slips, Setbacks, and Relapses

Despite your best efforts to work toward recovering from your eating disorder, you may still experience slips, setbacks, or relapses along your journey, as Kiera has. *Slips* are those isolated instances of eating disordered behaviors or thoughts. Slips may occur once or twice, but you are able to refocus on recovery without such behaviors or thoughts becoming a consistent occurrence. *Setbacks*, on the other hand, are times when you reengage in eating disordered behaviors for a brief period of time; they do not result in significant deterioration of your physical or mental well-being. When setbacks persist and you are reengaged in eating disordered behaviors for a significant amount of time, or when your physical or mental well-being begins to deteriorate, we consider this a *relapse*.

As Kiera's situation highlights, recovery is rarely a linear process, and everyone's process is unique to them. Slips, setbacks, and even relapses are common in the recovery process. You may think of these lapses as steps backward that are ruining the progress you have made in your recovery. And you may feel hopeless when thinking of relapses as part of the recovery process. Despite how accurate these thoughts and attitudes may seem or feel to you, they are likely not true. Each slip is a time to learn more about yourself and your recovery, and you can use that knowledge to improve and strengthen your recovery moving forward. Further, the more effort you put into managing minor slips or setbacks, the more effective you will be at preventing a full-blown relapse.

Before continuing, it is important to reiterate that there is no "right way" to recover from anorexia. Everyone's journey is different, and no one's journey is perfect. If you expect perfection, then minor slips will seem like great failures and may feel overwhelming and tremendously discouraging. But if you accept that everyone engaged in the recovery process will confront obstacles and will experience minor setbacks along the way, you can plan for them and learn from them. As you move through this chapter, remember to maintain realistic expectations for yourself. Expect that recovery will take time. Expect to face challenges and setbacks. Expect to make adjustments to your treatment as you face new challenges over time.

Practicing Self-Awareness

As emphasized throughout this book, being honest with yourself and your treatment team is an important part of recovery. This is not always easy, as anorexia is an ego-syntonic mental illness, often involving denial and inaccurate perceptions of one's own body, thoughts, behaviors, and emotions (see chapter 7 for further discussion on the ego-syntonic nature of anorexia). Thus, striving for self-awareness by being curious about, questioning, and understanding your motivations, actions, thoughts, and emotional experiences can help you catch yourself before falling further into your eating disorder. The sooner you are able to recognize you are slipping back into old patterns, the easier it will be to get yourself out of them.

There are several ways to foster self-awareness, which you can practice and use to recognize instances when you slip or experience a setback. Below are descriptions of each strategy. Take time to try each one, reflect on your experiences, and discuss what you notice with your psychotherapist. These strategies do not work instantly—you will begin to notice greater success the more you practice them.

Mindfulness

Briefly mentioned in several chapters so far, mindfulness is a practice and a way of being in the world. Through mindfulness, you create space between you and your judgments to notice and observe your mind and body. By taking a nonjudgmental and objective stance, you are better able to recognize your internal experiences, fostering self-awareness. There are hundreds of ways to practice mindfulness. Some examples you can try are described below.

Using Your Five Senses. Paying attention to your senses can be a grounding and present-focused activity to help you be mindful and in the moment. There are several ways to engage your senses mindfully:

- Choose one of your senses to focus on. Notice ten things with that sense while tuning out stimuli from other senses. For example, close your eyes and focus on listening. Identify ten different sounds you hear in your environment.

- Alternate your attention to different senses. While you sit, lie, or walk around, identify five things you feel, hear, and see. If you are around scents or tastes, include those senses as well.

- Use your senses during everyday activities. Instead of mindlessly washing the dishes, folding your clothes, or driving, notice what each of your different senses picks up on as you engage in these activities.

Observing Your Thoughts. Sit in a quiet room with your eyes closed. Let your mind think or do whatever it wants. Notice each thought and feeling that comes up and imagine placing each one on a leaf that is floating along a river. Observe your thoughts being carried away by the current. If you need something to ground you or help you focus, you can always attend to your breath. Do not change your breathing, just simply notice and experience it.

Using a Focal Object. Look at and focus on a single object, such as a flower or a candle. Take in everything you can about that object. Notice how your mind wanders, and when you observe your thoughts getting off track, bring your focus back to the object. Do this exercise for five to ten minutes. After completing the activity, reflect on what you noticed.

Relaxation

Mindfulness and relaxation techniques are often confused or referred to interchangeably. However, the goals of the two practices are quite different. In mindfulness, the goal is to be aware, while through relaxation you aim to feel relief from distress. Sometimes we are unable to be self-aware because intense emotions are interfering with our ability to be objective and responsive, leaving us emotionally invested and reactive. At those times, relaxation techniques may help you to get to a place psychologically, emotionally, and physically where you can practice skills that foster self-awareness. Below are some commonly helpful strategies for relaxation:

Diaphragmatic Breathing. Diaphragmatic breathing is a simple way to calm your body. By calming yourself physically, you can calm yourself mentally, as your mind and body are very much connected in relation to stress and distress. When we are breathing normally, we tend to take shallow breaths. Try these steps to help you breathe deeply to initiate a calming response:

- Sit or lie down in a comfortable position. Place one hand on your chest and one hand on your stomach.

- Breathe in slowly through your nose. You should feel your stomach move out against your hand while your chest remains still. Breathe in as much air as you can.

- Hold your breath for three seconds.

- Tighten your stomach muscles as you slowly breathe out through your mouth.

- Repeat these steps five times.

Progressive Muscle Relaxation (PMR). PMR is another way to physically relax your body to help ease tension and distress (Jacobson 1938). To complete this exercise, you tighten and release various muscle groups in your body. You can choose to go through your body from head to toe, as described below, or you can focus on the areas of your body where you feel your emotions.

In a quiet place, sit or lie in a comfortable position and close your eyes. Focus your mind on the sensations you feel by tightening and releasing your muscles. Try to let go of any other thoughts or distractions you notice. Tense each of the following muscle groups for five seconds, and then relax:

Forehead—Wrinkle your forehead, drawing your eyebrows toward your hairline. Notice the tension for five seconds. Relax.

Nose—Wrinkle your nose upward, as if smelling something unpleasant. Notice the tension for five seconds. Relax.

Cheeks—Smile as big as you can while tightening your cheeks. Notice the tension for five seconds. Relax.

Mouth—With your mouth closed, tighten your jaw by clenching your teeth. Notice the tension for five seconds. Relax.

Shoulders—Lift your shoulders as close to your ears as possible. Notice the tension for five seconds. Relax.

Arms—Flex your muscles tightly in your biceps and forearms. Notice the tension for five seconds. Relax.

Hands—Clench your fists tightly, as if you are squeezing the juice out of a lemon. Notice the tension for five seconds. Relax.

Back—Arch your back while keeping your shoulders back. Notice the tension for five seconds. Relax.

Stomach—Flex your stomach as if you are preparing for a heavy animal to step on it. Notice the tension for five seconds. Relax.

Legs—Squeeze your thighs and calves as hard as you can. Notice the tension for five seconds. Relax.

Feet—Bend your ankles to bring your toes up toward your body. Notice the tension for five seconds. Relax.

Toes—Curl your toes as tightly as possible. Notice the tension for five seconds. Relax.

Notice the tension leaving your body. Observe the sense of relaxation you feel. Gently bring your attention back to the room. When you are ready, open your eyes.

Imagery. Imagery can also help with relaxation. You can use imagery on your own or listen to audio recordings of guided imagery on your phone or computer. When using imagery, close your eyes and visualize a relaxing environment, such as a beach, a mountaintop, or driving with your windows down on an open road. Imagine yourself in that scenario and create as much detail as you can. Imagine what you would see, noticing the colors and textures of each item. Imagine what sounds you would hear. Imagine what pleasant things you could smell and taste. Imagine yourself touching things in your scene, taking notice of how they feel in your hands.

My Self-Awareness Practice

Take time to practice each technique and reflect on what you notice. You can use the chart on the next page to keep track of your self-awareness practice and to get a sense of which techniques are most helpful for you. It is important to remember that self-awareness strategies like mindfulness and relaxation techniques take time and practice. You may not feel an immediate effect, but continue to try different ways until you find one that helps you become more aware of the present moment, your mind, and your body. This chart is also available at http://www.newhar binger.com/39348.

Technique	When did you practice?	How long did you practice?	What did you notice?	How would you rate this technique?
Using Your Five Senses				
Observing Your Thoughts				
Using a Focal Object				
Diaphragmatic Breathing				
Progressive Muscle Relaxation				
Imagery				

Knowing Your Triggers

Before considering ways to deal with setbacks, let's discuss potential causes for an increase in eating disordered symptoms. Throughout this book, particularly in chapter 6, we have discussed the importance of identifying and effectively dealing with your triggers—the people, images, situations, behaviors, emotions, thoughts, discussions, or comments that elicit or increase your urges engage in eating disordered behaviors and thoughts. However, we have not yet explicitly explored what triggers you. Let's take some time to reflect on and list your specific triggers. These can include situations you encounter on a daily basis, things that have triggered you in the past, or things that you believe could be triggering in the future. Kiera has listed two of her main triggers below to get you started.

- *Hearing about my friends' fitness routines.*

- *Watching my friends get only "healthy" foods when we go out, while I'm trying to eat more things that scare me.*

- _____

- _____

- _____

- _____

- _____

Recognizing the Signs

Although you may not be able to avoid setbacks or relapses completely, there are steps you can take to lessen their frequency and severity, which can help you get back on track with recovery-oriented thoughts and actions. Kiera's profile described how she felt her relapses had come on almost overnight, without much warning. Like her, you sometimes might feel a relapse has sneaked up on you. This experience typically happens because you miss the warning signs that could have signaled early on that you were slipping. In reality, relapses do not happen overnight. There are often many slips (isolated instances of eating disordered behaviors or thoughts) or setbacks (periods of time during which you continued to engage in eating disordered behaviors and thoughts) that lead up to a relapse. Often, once you are in a relapse, self-awareness is not enough to help you fully refocus on recovery. Thus, it is important to recognize your triggers, slips, and setbacks early on, as these are the most effective times to intervene.

Using self-awareness and being honest with yourself, let's take inventory of your behaviors and thought patterns that may signal that you are slipping or experiencing a setback. To help you compile your list of warning signs, answer the following questions.

1.   What are your typical eating disordered symptoms and behaviors that may serve as a signal that you are struggling?

Kiera: *I withdraw from my family and friends, I sleep to avoid my feelings, and I increase my level of exercise.*

You: _____

_____

_____

2.   What signs have you or others noticed during past relapses?

Kiera: *People notice that I start to isolate more. Most people do not recognize my increased exercise, because I hide it from them.*

You: _____

_____

_____

3.   What behaviors or thoughts would concern you if you observed them in a friend?

Kiera: *I would be concerned if a friend stopped spending time with me and started avoiding contact with me. I would also be troubled if she was losing weight and got too thin.*

You: _____

_____

_____

4. What behaviors or thoughts typically or quickly escalate into habits for you (e.g., addictive behaviors like weighing yourself or exercising)?

Kiera: *Exercise is a slippery slope for me. It starts as just running an extra mile, and before I know it I'm running every day for way more miles than I should.*

You: _____

_____

_____

5. What excuses or rationalizations do you find yourself using or have you used in the past to dismiss eating disordered behaviors or thought patterns?

Kiera: *I tell myself that exercise is healthy and makes me feel good. I fail to admit or recognize when my behavior has moved to an unhealthy range.*

You: _____

_____

_____

6. What are some changes in you that others may notice that may be a warning sign that you are struggling?

Kiera: *I spend more time away from others: sleeping, exercising, and refusing to meet them (especially when food is involved). Along those same lines, I become more secretive and, because of my increased shame about relapse, I become more irritable, because I don't want people to point out that I'm not doing well.*

You: _____

_____

_____

7.   What are some behaviors or thoughts that you may be quick to dismiss as not meaningful, not relevant to your eating disorder, or not a big deal (e.g., engaging in rituals, body checking, negative self-talk)?

Kiera: *I quickly make excuses for and dismiss concerns about isolating and increased exercise. I tell myself that I'm too busy to spend time with others, when in reality I'm too ashamed to see them and busy doing unhealthy behaviors like overexercising and sleeping.*

You: _____

_____

_____

As you review your responses, keep in mind this list is not all-inclusive; it can change. The further you get into recovery, the more items will likely be on your list. For example, if counting calories or weighing yourself daily are currently behaviors you struggle with and are working on in your recovery, doing them would not indicate a slip or setback. However, once you conquer these behaviors and have abstained from them for a while or have engaged in them less frequently, an increase in these behaviors on a daily basis would be a warning sign for you. You may want to consider sharing this list with members of your treatment team and support system. This can help you both; you can gather their input and ideas now and they can be informed of the signs that you are struggling.

Be Accountable

It is easy to make excuses; minimize or dismiss signs of struggle; or keep your behaviors, thoughts, and emotions hidden from others. Unfortunately, secrets only serve to keep you sick. Despite how "wrong" or scary it feels to be vulnerable and honest, being accountable for your slips and struggles both to yourself and to your treatment team is important. Earlier in this chapter, you identified signs that you are slipping. Now, take a moment to list several people to whom you can commit to being accountable in your Relapse Prevention Plan, which is at the end of the chapter.

It may be helpful to ask people in your support system to check in routinely with you regarding setbacks. In order to open the discussion, you can request that a friend ask you every week, "What are you struggling with most this week?" It may feel forced at first, but with time it can become a fruitful way to maintain accountability. With your treatment team, you may want to request that sessions be structured in a way that gives you time in the beginning to identify your successes and struggles for the week, as well as the things you need to be held accountable for. By creating a routine that welcomes this type of vulnerability, you are more likely to be forthcoming and honest about your struggles.

Before moving on, let's take some time to be accountable right now. What is something related to your eating disorder recovery that you have struggled with in the past week? Examples can include weighing yourself more than you agreed to with your treatment team, excessive movement or exercise, or skipping breakfast. Below, write the things that you need to be held accountable for this week, and consider sharing them with your psychotherapist or a friend.

_____

_____

_____

Know When You Need More Help

Sometimes you may find yourself struggling to get back on track with your recovery. When you are in a good place in your recovery, take time with your treatment team to determine what would be indicators of needing increased support—and what kind of increased support you might first turn to (e.g., increased frequency of sessions, attending an intensive outpatient program). This can be informal or in the form of a written contract. While it may feel scary or seem childish to have a written contract, it can be immensely helpful when you are slipping and your eating disordered thoughts, rather than your logical thoughts, are more prominent. If you and your psychotherapist feel that a therapeutic contract can help to keep you safe and in recovery, you may want to use the following sample therapeutic contract as a model. This contract is also available at http://www.newharbinger.com/39348.

Sample Therapeutic Contract

Date:_____

I, _____ , agree to the following terms of my treatment. My treatment team and I have agreed upon the following expectations in order to continue my treatment on an outpatient basis:

- _____

- _____

- _____

We also agree that if any of the following events occur, I will increase the frequency of my outpatient treatment:

- _____

- _____

- _____

My treatment team and I agree that I must seek a higher level of care if any of the following events occur:

- _____

- _____

- _____

Signed,

_____ (patient)

_____ (psychotherapist)

_____ (dietitian)

_____ (physician)

Not all slips require more support or a higher level of care. However, if you do not identify a line that, when it is crossed, indicates you do need more intense or more frequent treatment, you are likely to intervene too late. While these lines may seem arbitrary, they are necessary boundaries for you to set for yourself in order to prevent or lessen the severity of a lapse.

A common line that is drawn relates to your weight. You and your treatment team may agree that you need to maintain a weight above a certain point in order to continue at the current frequency of your outpatient treatment. Losing weight is certainly a helpful and tangible indicator that you are struggling to maintain your health and your recovery. However, there are many other lines that can be made related to your behaviors, thinking, emotions, and activities of daily living. For example, if you find you are purging more than once per week, having suicidal thoughts, feeling depressed, or isolating yourself socially, it might a sign of a serious struggle.

What are the lines that, if crossed, indicate that you may be slipping toward relapse and that you need more support? Make these lines specific and measurable, similar to the process of creating SMART goals from chapter 6. Write your ideas below and discuss them with your treatment team. You can then modify them, if needed, based on the feedback you receive from your treatment team.

_____

_____

_____

Ask for Help

Once you realize that you need more help, you may need to ask for it. Even with a treatment contract in place, you may find that your team does not immediately notice the indicators that you need help. Asking for help can be extremely difficult, especially when you are in the vulnerable state of needing increased support. But try to remember that needing help and asking for it are not signs of failure. Recovery is quite a bumpy road, and everyone needs support along the way.

It can be helpful to identify individuals ahead of time whom you can approach to ask for more help when needed, such as your parents, friends, and treatment team members. Whom would you feel most comfortable telling you are struggling and need more support? What form of communication would you most like to use (talking face-to-face, writing an e-mail, texting)? How would you like for that person to respond or help that is in line with your recovery goals? Write your ideas in the chart on the next page and share this information with the people you identify so they can understand effective and helpful ways to respond. See Kiera's responses below for guidance in completing your chart. This chart is also available at http://www.newharbinger.com/39348.

With whom can you talk?	How will you communicate?	How can they respond?
My therapist	I will tell her what I'm struggling with, or I will write it down if talking seems too hard in the moment.	I will need her to validate my emotions first and not jump into problem solving right away.
My best friend	I will text her if I need her support.	She can ask me what I need from her in the moment that would be helpful.

Refocus on Your Values and Use Committed Action

Whether you continue to work on managing a setback with your outpatient team or decide to seek a higher level of care, refocusing on your values in order to take committed action toward recovery is a necessary step in the process. During a setback, it may be tempting to continue acting on eating disordered thoughts and behaviors. Refocusing on recovery takes a lot of work and effort, and allowing yourself to fall deeper into a relapse often feels like the easier option. However, when you lose sight of recovery, you lose sight of your values. Relapse only takes you farther away from what makes your life meaningful. When you find yourself slipping, it can be helpful to remind yourself why you are fighting for recovery.

Take some time to complete the chart below to refer back to when you find yourself wanting to give up. List your values in the first column. In the second column, list ways recovery brings you closer to that value. Then identify ways relapsing will take you away from each value. This chart is also available at http://www.newharbinger.com/39348.

Value	In recovery, my actions have the following effect on my values:	In relapse, my actions have the following effect on my values:

Now take this activity a step further with committed action. *Living* your values, rather than simply *knowing* them, is a much more powerful experience and reminder of why you fight each day for recovery. What are some actions you can take to live closer to each of your values? These ideas can include both actions related to your eating disorder (e.g., calling a friend to eat dinner with you or joining an eating disorder support group) and actions that are not directly related to it (e.g., volunteering or joining a recreational sports league). List specific and realistic ideas or goals below.

_____

_____

_____

_____

_____

Use Your Skills

Focusing on your values and taking action to live closer to them may provide the necessary motivation to work toward getting back on track with your recovery, but doing so does not take away the distress and emotional toll that accompanies this process. Various strategies and techniques for dealing with difficulties you may encounter in recovery and in life have been discussed throughout this book, including communication skills, self-care, radical acceptance, daily thought records, relaxation, and mindfulness. All of these can assist you in some capacity in dealing with setbacks.

However, there is an array of coping skills that we have not yet discussed that can help to lessen and regulate your emotional reactions that can cause or be a result of experiencing setbacks in your recovery. Increased levels of distress will only prolong or worsen a lapse, and you will have difficulty problem solving when emotions are intense. It is important to learn to tolerate and cope with emotional reactions effectively.

There are many approaches to coping with distress and regulating your emotions. The following approaches represent just a handful of possible skills for you to try. With the help of your psychotherapist, explore each option and see which ones work best for you, as not every skill is helpful for each person. Also, remember that these skills do not solve the underlying problems that are causing you distress. They are used to help you manage your emotions so you can then take the necessary steps to problem solve with a clear mind.

Expansion

Expansion is an acceptance and commitment therapy skill in which you make room for unpleasant feelings (Hayes, Strosahl, and Wilson 2012). Normally when we experience an intense and painful emotion, the first reaction is to do everything we can to push it away. However, the more energy you put into pushing away the emotion, the more you are consumed by it. Rather than viewing a negative feeling as something that needs to be dispelled, try to accept all emotions as part of life—and part of *you*—and make room for them in your life.

Consider this metaphor: Imagine your emotions are a monster on the opposite side of a door trying to push its way into your room. You are using all of your strength to brace the door to keep it out. What are you thinking about? Most likely, all of your energy is centered on keeping the monster on the other side of the door. The more you fight the monster, the more it consumes your thoughts. Now imagine that instead of treating your emotions like a monster, you invited them inside, and you became friendly with them. They sit on your couch, and you feel their presence, but you are able to focus on other things, such as watching television or reading a book, because you made room for them. When we fight inevitable emotions, our struggle is actually counterproductive, because we are forcing our minds to think about them. If you can invite the emotions into your life, make room for them, and utilize a support system (family, friends, treatment team, coping skills, self-compassion), you no longer are hyper-focused on them and can go about your life more at ease.

Of course, emotional acceptance is easier said than done! Talk about this process of expansion with your psychotherapist, and use it in conjunction with other effective coping skills you have learned.

Urge Surfing

Urge surfing is a skill in which you wait out your urges to act on unhealthy behaviors (Marlatt and Gordon 1985; Harris 2008). When having urges to act on eating disordered behaviors, try riding them like a wave. Like intense emotions, urges will not last forever; they all will pass. Like a wave, urges increase in intensity and eventually decrease. Mindfully observe your urge and rate it on a scale of 0 to 10, with higher numbers indicating stronger urges. Do not try to distract yourself from the urge. Instead, engage in a values-oriented or self-care activity and notice your urge coming and going. Take note of your rating of the urge as you are waiting for it to pass, and reflect on the following questions. How long did it take to decrease by half? What did you notice in your body as you waited the urge out? How do you feel now that the urge has passed?

Self-Soothe

Taking time to engage each of your senses in a mindful way can decrease distress (Johnson 1985; Linehan 1993). Create a self-soothe kit that you can access when you are upset. In a box or bag, place items that relate to each of your senses and that you find soothing. Below are some ideas for each sense. In the space below each sense, write down what you can include in your own self-soothe kit for that specific sense.

- *Touch*—a soft piece of fabric, putty, a stress ball

  For my self-soothe kit, I can include: _____

  _____

- *Smell*—a candle, perfume, essential oils

  For my self-soothe kit, I can include: _____

  _____

- *Taste*—gum, chocolate, tea, a piece of candy

  For my self-soothe kit, I can include: _____

  _____

- *Sight*—pictures of friends or family, a drawing, a calming scene

  For my self-soothe kit, I can include: _____

  _____

- *Hearing*—music, guided meditation, a voicemail from a loved one

  For my self-soothe kit, I can include: _____

  _____

Do the Opposite of Your Emotional Urges

When we feel emotions, we often have a typical way we want to respond. If you are angry, you may want to yell at someone; if you are sad, you may want to watch a sad movie. Sometimes experiencing the emotion fully allows the distress to be released, and you begin to feel like you are back at baseline. Other times, however, engaging in activities that elicit your painful emotions exacerbates your emotions and increases your distress. When this happens it may be helpful to do something that elicits the opposite emotion than what you are feeling (Linehan 1993). In other words, do the opposite of your initial emotional urges. If you are feeling angry, engage in relaxation activities instead of hitting something or yelling. If you are feeling sad, listen to upbeat music instead of depressing songs. See Kiera's example immediately below. Then, complete the activity that follows to illustrate how you can do the opposite of your emotional urges. This exercise is also available at http://www.newharbinger.com/39348.

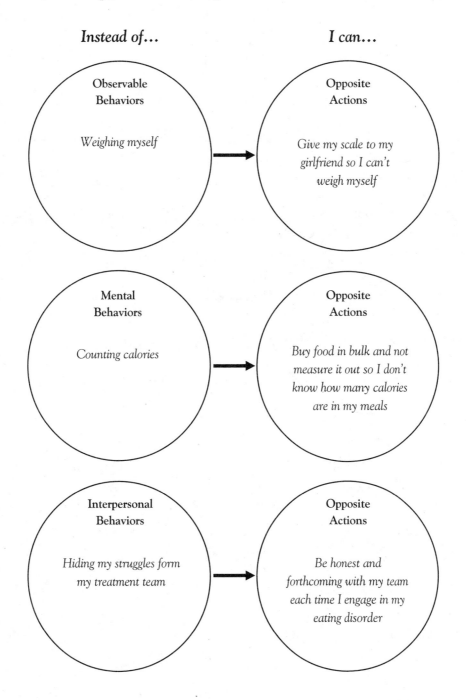

Instead of...   *I can...*

Observable Behaviors

Weighing myself

Opposite Actions

Give my scale to my girlfriend so I can't weigh myself

Mental Behaviors

Counting calories

Opposite Actions

Buy food in bulk and not measure it out so I don't know how many calories are in my meals

Interpersonal Behaviors

Hiding my struggles form my treatment team

Opposite Actions

Be honest and forthcoming with my team each time I engage in my eating disorder

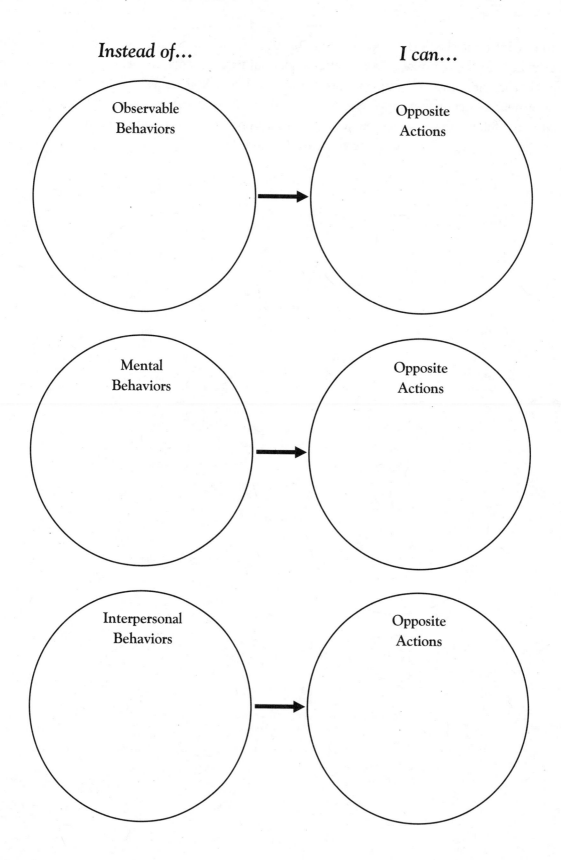

Get Active and Distract

When you are burdened by painful emotions, get up and do something! Engage in activities that can distract you from and ease your pain. There are many ways to lessen your distress through action:

- Engage in activities that you find pleasant and enjoyable, such as reading a book, listening to music, taking a walk, or drinking coffee. Review your work on self-care from chapter 11 or ideas on what activities you find pleasurable.

- Do something that helps with emotional expression, such as journaling, painting, or squeezing a stress ball.

- Use distractions to help remove yourself from a painful emotion or situation. Try counting backward from one hundred by threes, blowing bubbles, or watching television.

- Move your body to let off steam. Go for a walk, do yoga, or stretch.

- Socialize—call or meet up with a friend to help you remember you are not alone.

What are ten ways you can actively distract yourself? Create a list in the space below and feel free to add to it. The more distraction techniques you can list, the better. When you are in need of some distraction, review this list and choose one. If it is not helping you, move down the list until you find one that is effective in that moment.

1. _____

2. _____

3. _____

4. _____

5. _____

6. _____

7. _____

8. _____

9. _____

10. _____

Deal with Self-Defeating Thoughts

Thoughts that can detract from your recovery and progress often come up throughout recovery. These self-defeating thoughts can be in the form of self-deprecation (*I'm worthless.*), predictions about your recovery (*There is no way I will ever fully recovery, so why try?*), or eating disordered ways of thinking (*I need to purge just this one time, and then I will stop.*). While you may not be able to completely get rid of these types of thoughts, it is important to learn to manage them when they pop up. In the following pages we provide a variety of skills for you to try. Review them with your psychotherapist and keep practicing them. With practice, they will become more natural and helpful.

Dialectical Thinking

In DBT, thinking dialectically means that two things that may seem very different—or even opposites—can be true at the same time (Linehan 1993). When you are faced with self-defeating thoughts, try to also acknowledge ways that you are doing well. For example, you may be thinking, *I am never going to recover.* To combat this, try changing this statement to *I am currently feeling hopeless about recovery, and I am capable of making healthy choices that will move me forward in my recovery.* Notice the use of the word "and." It may feel more natural to use the word "but"; however, using "but" indicates that you are negating or invalidating the first part of the statement. Remember that you can feel hopeless and hopeful at the same time. Both sentiments can be true. Practice reframing self-defeating thoughts in such a way that validates your current feelings and fosters dialectical thinking, such that you can feel negatively about yourself and find positives in yourself at the same time. Follow these three steps to complete the chart below:

1. Identify a self-defeating thought.

2. State and validate the feelings you have associated with that statement.

3. Complete your sentence by stating a positive or logical fact associated with your original thought, using the word "and" as your conjunction to connect steps 2 and 3.

The goal is to acknowledge the emotions related to or driving your self-defeating thoughts while also challenging the thought to be more well-rounded and based in reality by acknowledging the simultaneous positive or logical aspects of the situation. For guidance, follow the example Kiera provided for you.

Original Thought	Validation of Current Feelings	And...
Kiera: *It is so embarrassing how many times I have relapsed and reentered treatment.*	*I'm feeling a lot of shame around my recovery journey...*	*and I know that my past behaviors do not have to dictate my future actions in recovery.*

Challenging and Reframing

Cognitive behavior therapy is strongly focused on changing your self-defeating thoughts. In chapter 7, we discussed using a daily thought record to record, label, challenge, and reframe cognitive distortions. If you need to, revisit chapter 7 to refresh your memory on how to challenge and reframe your thoughts. You may want to go back and add self-defeating thoughts related to recovery and relapse to your daily thought record.

Defusion

A core component of ACT is *cognitive defusion*, which is the practice of distancing yourself from your thoughts by observing them and letting them come and go rather than holding on to them. Thoughts are simply words, pictures, and stories. They do not hold meaning unless we give them meaning. We can observe our thoughts as just thoughts and not let them negatively impact us. A common phrase in ACT is "a thought is not an order." Your thoughts do not have to dictate how you feel and act. To practice defusion, try noticing your self-defeating thoughts and put the words "I'm having the thought that" in front of them. For example, instead of saying to herself, *I am never going to recover*, Kiera could practice defusion by stating, "I'm having the thought that I am never going to recover." Kiera could also create some distance from thoughts like *I need to restrict* by stating, *I notice I am having the urge to restrict*. What are some thoughts you have that can be altered to help you defuse from them?

Instead of Thinking...	I Can Say...
Kiera: *Everyone should give up on me because I will never recover.*	*I'm having the thought that everyone should give up on me because I will never recover.*

Another defusion technique is to label the stories that you tend to play in your head and, when you catch yourself replaying those unhelpful, self-defeating thoughts, notice them and say things such as, *Oh, there's my shame story again!* or *Thanks, mind, for reminding me of my failure story!* When you defuse from a thought, you are able to distance yourself from it, which gives it less power over you. You are more than your thoughts. What are some stories that often play in your head that are not helpful for you or your recovery? What could you call each story so you are better able to defuse from it when it pops up?

Things I Often Tell Myself	This Story Can Be Called...
Kiera: *Because I relapsed in the past there is no way I will ever be able to fully recover.*	*This is my "Never Gonna Do It" story.*

Practice Self-Compassion

As mentioned earlier, setbacks and lapses in your recovery are common and often part of the process. As Kiera expressed, shame and guilt over these hard times is a common experience in recovery. But just as it is unhelpful to give up in response to this reality, it is also unhelpful to beat yourself up for slipping. Recovery is rarely, if ever, a linear process. Try to be compassionate toward yourself by remembering these three components of self-compassion: kindness, common humanity, and mindfulness (Neff 2003).

Kindness

Be warm and understanding toward yourself. Rather than beating yourself up, talk to and comfort yourself the way you would talk to a friend. How can you practice kindness toward yourself today?

_____

_____

_____

Common Humanity

Setbacks, failures, and imperfections are part of life. Recognize that we, as humans, are imperfect and that we are not alone in our suffering. What are some statements you can say to remind yourself that negative experiences are a normal part of life?

_____

_____

_____

Mindfulness

Notice and accept your negative emotions and painful experiences as they are, without avoiding or overly attaching to them. List some ways you have learned to help you practice mindfulness when you are experiencing painful thoughts and feelings?

_____

_____

_____

Sharing My Relapse Prevention Plan

We have emphasized throughout this chapter that everyone's recovery journey is different. The one thing that seems to be universal to eating disorder recovery is that you cannot do it alone. Support is a necessary part of recovery. Sharing your plan for recognizing and managing lapses in your recovery can be useful because the plan informs others of how and when they can help you. Complete the chart below to identify who you want involved in your efforts for preventing relapses. Include details regarding how each person can help you in this process. Then go and talk with the people listed and tell them how they can best support you.

People I Want Involved	How They Can Best Help Me

Congratulations!

As you approach the end of this book, we want to thank you for taking this journey through the workbook with us and for involving us in your recovery process. Congratulations on getting this far, and we hope that this workbook has been helpful for you. We encourage you to revisit this workbook throughout your recovery, because as you move along in this journey it will be important to reflect on the past in order to improve your future. You may find that some of your answers to exercises remain the same, while others may change, based on where you are in recovery. Continue using this workbook as long as you find it helpful for you. We wish you nothing but the best in your recovery and life and appreciate your efforts in healing.

Journaling Pages

In this chapter, we discussed how slips, setbacks, and relapses are common in recovery from anorexia. We also addressed the importance of self-awareness, knowing your triggers and warning signs, being accountable, asking for help, focusing on values and committed actions, using coping skills, and practicing self-compassion in eating disorder recovery. Use the space below to take some time to reflect on your progress in your recovery as you have worked through the exercises in this book. How has your recovery and well-being improved since beginning this workbook? How have you managed any slips, setbacks, or relapses? What skills or topics in this book do you think may be helpful to revisit?

_____

_____

_____

_____

_____

_____

_____

_____

_____

_____

_____

_____

Acknowledgments

There were a number of individuals at New Harbinger who helped us to take this book from an idea to the finished product you are now reading. We are indebted to them and would not have been able to write or produce this book without their expert guidance, support, and assistance. These include acquisitions editors Wendy Millstine, Melissa Valentine, and Elizabeth Hollis Hansen. These great colleagues helped us to better focus our ideas and expertly guided us through the publication process. We also express our appreciation to developmental editor Erin Raber, editorial manager Clancy Drake, editor Caleb Beckwith, and associate editor Vicraj Gill. They helped us to do our best work possible as we wrote this book. Finally, we are very appreciative of the work of copy editor Jennifer Eastman, whose attention to detail and great editing skill helped to make our writing even better. The writing and publishing of this book was a team effort, and we are greatly appreciative to each member of our team.

Catherine Ruscitti

Jeffrey Barnett

Rebecca Wagner

Resources

Eating disorders are complex and often misunderstood illnesses, which can make finding accurate information, treatment resources, and recovery-focused communities a difficult feat. Therefore, this appendix provides you with a compilation of international, national, and regional organizations dedicated to providing you with helpful information, such as information about eating disorders, treatment resources, eating disorder specialists, and support groups. As a disclaimer, no endorsement is being provided for the resources listed below. Each link is included as a representative example of available resources to help you gather information to help determine if a particular resource would be beneficial for you. You may wish to review these resources with members of your treatment team to determine which are likely to be the most relevant for you.

Additionally, this list is not exhaustive, and available resources can change over time. For example, in the regional resources below, some states do not have an active website for eating disorder resources (and, thus, are not listed); however, this can change. Therefore, it may be useful for you to also utilize Internet search engines, using keywords such as "eating disorder providers near [insert city]" or "eating disorder resources in [insert state]," to locate additional resources.

International Resources

Academy for Eating Disorders
http://aedweb.org

Eating Disorder Referral and Information Center
http://www.edreferral.com

Families Empowered and Supporting Treatment of Eating Disorders (FEAST)
http://members.feast-ed.org

International Association of Eating Disorders Professionals Foundation
http://iaedp.site-ym.com/search/custom.asp?id=4255

National Resources

The Alliance for Eating Disorders Awareness
http://www.allianceforeatingdisorders.com

American Psychological Association
http://locator.apa.org

Eating Disorder Hope
http://www.eatingdisorderhope.com

Eating Disorders Anonymous (EDA)
http://www.eatingdisordersanonymous.org

Eating Disorders Resource Catalogue
http://www.edcatalogue.com

Eating Disorders Recovery Today
http://www.eatingdisordersrecoverytoday.com

Eat Right
http://www.eatright.org

The Elisa PROJECT
http://www.theelisaproject.org

International Federation of Eating Disorder Dietitians
http://www.eddietitians.com

MentorCONNECT
http://www.mentorconnect-ed.org

My Eating Disorder Centers
http://www.myeatingdisordercenters.com

National Association of Anorexia Nervosa and Associated Disorders (ANAD)
http://www.anad.org

National Eating Disorder Association (NEDA)
http://www.nationaleatingdisorders.org

Project HEAL
http://www.theprojectheal.org

Psychology Today
http://www.psychologytoday.com

Residential Eating Disorders Consortium (REDC)
http://www.residentialeatingdisorders.org/our-members

Something Fishy
http://www.something-fishy.org

Therapytribe
http://www.therapytribe.com

Theravive
http://www.theravive.com

Regional Resources

Alabama

Alabama Network for Eating Disorders Awareness
http://www.alabamaeatingdisorders.com/index.php

California

Eating Disorders Resource Center (EDRC)
http://www.edrcsv.org

Colorado

The Eating Disorder Foundation
http://www.eatingdisorderfoundation.org

Florida

The Alliance for Eating Disorders Awareness
http://www.allianceforeatingdisorders.com

The Eating Disorder Network of Central Florida
http://www.edncf.com

Georgia

Eating Disorders Information Network (EDIN)
http://www.myedin.org

Indiana

Eating Disorders Task Force of Indiana (EDTF)
http://www.edtfi.org/?membership.html

Iowa

Eating Disorder Coalition of Iowa (EDCI)
http://www.edciowa.com

Kentucky

Eating Disorders Coalition of Kentuckiana
https://nortonhealthcare.com/pages/eating-disorders-coalition.aspx

Maine

Eating Disorders Association of Maine (EDAM)
http://maineeatingdisorders.org

Maryland

Eating Disorder Network of Maryland (also includes Washington DC and Northern Virginia)
http://www.ednmaryland.org

Massachusetts

Multi-Service Eating Disorders Association (MEDA)
http://www.medainc.org

Michigan

Michigan Eating Disorders Alliance (MIEDA)
http://www.mieda.org

Southwest Michigan Eating Disorders Association (SMEDA)
http://www.southwestmichiganeatingdisorders.org

Missouri

Missouri Eating Disorders Association
http://moeatingdisorders.org

New York

Ulster County Eating Disorders Coalition (EDC)
http://www.eatingdisordersny.com

Eating Disorders Recovery Center of Western New York
http://www.nyeatingdisorders.org

North Carolina

T.H.E. Center for Disordered Eating of Western North Carolina
http://www.thecenternc.org/index.html

Oklahoma

Oklahoma Eating Disorders Association (OEDA)
http://www.okeatingdisorders.org

Oregon

Columbia River Eating Disorder Network (also includes Washington)
http://www.credn.org

Pennsylvania

The Pennsylvania Educational Network for Eating Disorders (PENED)
http://www.pened.org/index.html

American Anorexia and Bulimia Association of Philadelphia (AABA)
http://www.aabaphila.org

Tennessee

MCR Foundation: For the Prevention of Eating Disorders
http://www.mcrfoundation.com

A Place of Healing: An Eating Disorder Resource Center
http://www.healingtn.org

Renewed: Eating Disorder Support (Formerly Eating Disorders Coalition of Tennessee)
http://www.edct.net

Texas

Austin Eating Disorders Specialists (AEDS)
http://austineds.com

Houston Eating Disorders Specialists
http://www.houstoneds.org

Virginia

Eating Disorder Network of Southwest Virginia
http://www.eatingdisorders-swva.org

Washington, DC

Rock Recovery (also Maryland and Virginia)
http://rockrecoveryed.org

References

American Psychiatric Association. 2013. *Diagnostic and Statistical Manual of Mental Disorders.* 5th ed. Arlington, VA: American Psychiatric Association.

Arcelus, J., A. J. Mitchell, J. Wales, and S. Nielsen. 2011. "Mortality Rates in Patients with Anorexia Nervosa and Other Eating Disorders: A Meta-Analysis of 36 Studies." *Archives of General Psychiatry* 68: 724–731.

Bandura, A. 1977. "Self-Efficacy: Toward a Unifying Theory of Behavioral Change." *Psychological Review* 84: 191–215.

Bankoff, S. M., M. G. Karpel, H. E. Forbes, and D. W. Pantalone. 2012. "A Systematic Review of Dialectical Behavior Therapy for the Treatment of Eating Disorders." *Eating Disorders* 20: 196–215.

Baumeister, R. F., and M. R. Leary. 1995. "The Need to Belong: Desire for Interpersonal Attachments as a Fundamental Human Motivation." *Psychological Bulletin* 117: 497–529.

Beck, J. S. 2011. *Cognitive Behavior Therapy: Basics and Beyond.* New York: Guilford Press.

Berkman, N. D., C. M. Bulik, K. A. Brownley, K. N. Lohr, J. A. Sedway, A. Rooks, and G. Garlehner. 2006. *Management of Eating Disorders. Evidence Report/Technology Assessment No. 135* (Prepared by the RTI International University of North Carolina Evidence-Based Practice Center under Contract No. 290–02–0016) AHRQ Publication No. 06-E010. Rockville, MD: Agency for Healthcare Research and Quality.

Berman, M. I., K. N. Boutelle, and S. J. Crow. 2009. "A Case Series Investigating Acceptance and Commitment Therapy as a Treatment for Previously Treated, Unremitted Patients with Anorexia Nervosa." *European Eating Disorders Review* 17: 426–434.

Brown, B. 2010. *The Gifts of Imperfection: Let Go of Who You Think You're Supposed to Be and Embrace Who You Are.* Center City, MN: Hazelden Publishing.

Bulik, C. M., P. F. Sullivan, F. Tozzi, H. Furberg, P. Lichtenstein, and N. L. Pedersen. 2006. "Prevalence, Heritability, and Prospective Risk Factors for Anorexia Nervosa." *Archives of General Psychiatry* 63: 305–312.

Bulik, C. M., L. Thornton, T. L. Root, E. M. Pisetsky, P. Lichtenstein, and N. L. Pedersen. 2010. "Understanding the Relation Between Anorexia Nervosa and Bulimia Nervosa in a Swedish National Twin Sample." *Biological Psychiatry* 67: 71–77.

Cockell, S. J., S. L. Zaitsoff, and J. Geller. 2004. "Maintaining Change Following Eating Disorder Treatment." *Professional Psychology: Research and Practice* 35: 527–534.

Couturier, J., and J. Lock. 2006. "What Is Recovery in Adolescent Anorexia Nervosa." *International Journal of Eating Disorders* 39: 550–555.

Crocker, J., and L. E. Park. 2003. "Seeking Self-Esteem: Construction, Maintenance, and Protection of Self-Worth." In *Handbook of Self and Identity*, edited by M. Leary and J. Tangney, 291–313. New York: Guilford Press.

Crow, S., B. Praus, and P. Thuras. 1999. "Mortality from Eating Disorders: A Five- to Ten-Year Record Linkage Study." *International Journal of Eating Disorders* 26: 97–101.

Darcy, A. M., S. Katz, K. K. Fitzpatrick, S. Forsberg, L. Utzinger, and J. Lock. 2010. "All Better: How Former Anorexia Nervosa Patients Define Recovery and Engaged in Treatment." *European Eating Disorder Review* 18: 260–270.

Doran, G. T. 1981. "There's a S.M.A.R.T. Way to Write Management's Goals and Objectives." *Management Review* 70: 35.

Federici, A., and A. S. Kaplan. 2008. "The Patient's Account of Relapse and Recovery in Anorexia Nervosa: A Qualitative Study." *European Eating Disorders Review* 16: 1–10.

Galsworthy-Francis, L., and S. Allan. 2014. "Cognitive Behavioural Therapy for Anorexia Nervosa: A Systematic Review." *Clinical Psychology Review* 34: 54–72.

Granek, L. 2007. "'You're a Whole Lot of Person': Understanding the Journey Through Anorexia to Recovery: A Qualitative Study." *Humanistic Psychologist* 35: 363–385.

Guarda, A. S. 2008. "Treatment of Anorexia Nervosa: Insights and Obstacles." *Physiological Behavior* 94: 113–120

Harris, R. 2008. *The Happiness Trap: How to Stop Struggling and Start Living*. Boston: Trumpeter Books.

Hayes, S. C., K. D. Strosahl, and K. G. Wilson. 2012. *Acceptance and Commitment Therapy: The Process and Practice of Mindful Change*. 2nd ed. New York: Guilford Press.

Herzog, D. B., D. N. Greenwood, D. J. Dorer, A. T. Flores, E. R. Ekeblad, A. Richards, M. A. Blais, and M. B. Keller. 2000. "Mortality in Eating Disorders: A Descriptive Study." *International Journal of Eating Disorders* 28: 20–26.

Hudson, J. I., E. Hiripi, H. G. Pope, and R. C. Kessler. 2007. "The Prevalence and Correlates of Eating Disorders in the National Comorbidity Survey Replication." *Biological Psychiatry* 61: 348–358.

Jacobson, E. 1938. *Progressive Relaxation.* Chicago: University of Chicago Press.

Johnson, S. M. 1985. *Characterological Transformation: The Hard Work Miracle.* New York: W. W. Norton.

Juarascio, A., J. Shaw, E. Forman, C. A. Timko, J. Herbert, M. Butryn, D. Bunnell, A. Matteucci, and M. Lowe. 2013. "Acceptance and Commitment Therapy as a Novel Treatment for Eating Disorders: An Initial Test of Efficacy and Mediation." *Behavior Modification* 37: 459–489.

Klump, K. L., J. L. Suisman, S. A. Burt, M. McGue, and W. G. Iacono. 2009. "Genetic and Environmental Influences on Disordered Eating: An Adoption Study." *Journal of Abnormal Psychology* 118: 797–805.

Linehan, M. M. (1993). *Cognitive-Behavioral Treatment of Borderline Personality Disorder.* New York: Guilford Press.

Mains, J. A., and F. R. Scogin. 2003. "The Effectiveness of Self-Administered Treatment: A Practice-Friendly Review of the Research." *Journal of Clinical Psychology* 59: 237–246.

Marlatt, G. A., and J. R. Gordon. 1985. *Relapse Prevention: Maintenance Strategies in the Treatment of Addictive Behaviors.* New York: Guilford Press.

Martin, J. B. 2010. "The Development of Ideal Body Image Perceptions in the United States." *Nutrition Today* 45: 98–100.

Maslow, A. H. 1943. "A Theory of Human Motivation." *Psychological Review* 50: 370–396.

McFarlane, T., M. P. Olmsted, and K. Trottier. 2008. "Timing and Prediction of Relapse in Transdiagnostic Eating Disorder Sample." *International Journal of Eating Disorders* 41: 587–593.

Miller, W. R., J. C'de Baca, D. B. Matthews, and P. L. Wilbourne. 2001. "Personal Values Card Sort." Retrieved from casaa.unm.edu/inst/Personal Values Card Sort.pdf.

Neff, K. 2003. "Self-Compassion: An Alternative Conceptualization of a Healthy Attitude Toward Oneself." *Self and Identity* 2: 85–101.

Nilsson, K., and B. Hagglof. 2006. "Patient Perspectives of Recovery in Adolescent Onset Anorexia Nervosa." *Eating Disorders* 14: 305–311.

Patching, J., and J. Lawler. 2009. "Understanding Women's Experiences of Developing an Eating Disorder and Recovering: A Life-History Approach." *Nursing Inquiry* 16: 10–21.

Polivy, J., and P. C. Herman. 2002. "Causes of Eating Disorders." *Annual Review of Psychology* 53: 187–213.

Prochaska, J. O., and W. F. Velicer. 1997. "The Transtheoretical Model of Health Behavior Change." *American Journal of Health Promotion* 12: 38–48.

Rosenberg, M. 1965. *Society and the Adolescent Self-Image*. Princeton, NJ: Princeton University Press.

Sandoz, E. K., K. G. Wilson, and T. DuFrene. 2010. *Acceptance and Commitment Therapy for Eating Disorders: A Process-Focused Guide to Treating Anorexia and Bulimia*. Oakland, CA: New Harbinger Publications.

Strober, M., R. Freeman, C. Lampert, J. Diamond, and W. Kaye. 2000. "Controlled Family Study of Anorexia Nervosa and Bulimia Nervosa: Evidence of Shared Liability and Transmission of Partial Syndromes." *American Journal of Psychiatry* 157: 393–401.

Sullivan, P. F. 1995. "Mortality in Anorexia Nervosa." *American Journal of Psychiatry* 152: 1073–1074.

Tozzi, F., P. F. Sullivan, J. L. Fear, J. McKenzie, and C. M. Bulik. 2003. "Causes and Recovery in Anorexia Nervosa: The Patient's Perspective." *International Journal of Eating Disorders* 33: 143–154.

Vanderlinden, J., H. Buis, G. Pieters, and M. Probst. 2007. "Which Elements in the Treatment of Eating Disorders Are Necessary Ingredients in the Recovery Process: A Comparison Between the Patient's and Therapist's View." *European Eating Disorders Review* 15: 357–365.

Wade, T. D., C. M. Bulik, M. Neale, and K. S. Kendler. 2001. "Anorexia Nervosa and Major Depression: Shared Genetic and Environmental Risk Factors." *American Journal of Psychiatry* 157: 469–471.

Waller, G., and H. Kennerley. 2003. "Cognitive-Behavioral Treatments." In *Handbook of Eating Disorders*, 2nd ed., edited by J. Treasure, U. Schmidt, and E. Furth 233–252. Chichester, England: Wiley.

Catherine L. Ruscitti, PsyD, is a licensed psychologist and primary therapist at the Eating Recovery Center of Houston. She completed her predoctoral and postdoctoral training with Baylor College of Medicine at The Menninger Clinic in Houston, TX. Ruscitti specializes in the assessment and treatment of adolescents and young adults with eating disorders and comorbid struggles, including mood disorders, anxiety and trauma, and personality disorders. Her professional interests include the use of acceptance and commitment therapy (ACT) in the treatment of eating disorders, and the role of emotion regulation in recovery from eating disorders. Ruscitti is active in conducting research on eating disorders, and has published several papers on the topic.

Jeffrey E. Barnett, PsyD, ABPP, is associate dean for graduate programs and the social sciences and professor in the department of psychology at Loyola University Maryland, and a licensed psychologist in independent practice in Baltimore, MD. He has given over 300 presentations and workshops for mental health professionals, and has over 200 publications in print and online. Barnett is widely published in ethics and professional practice issues for mental health professionals, with many of his books being written broadly for all mental health professionals—not just psychologists. Additionally, he has received numerous professional awards on the national level, and has presented regularly for decades at conferences for mental health professionals.

Rebecca A. Wagner, PhD, is clinical director of the Eating Recovery Center in Houston, TX. She is a voluntary faculty member at Baylor College of Medicine in the department of psychiatry and behavioral sciences. Prior to her role at the Eating Recovery Center of Houston, she was director of eating disorder services, and codeveloper of the Eating Disorder Track at The Menninger Clinic. She specializes in the assessment and treatment of eating disorders, as well as other complex mental disorders. Wagner actively conducts research, and teaches professionals and those in the community about eating disorders. She has given numerous presentations about eating disorders and has several publications on the topic. Wagner's professional interests include the efficacy of an innovative approach to the treatment of eating disorders, body dissatisfaction, emotion dysregulation, self-harm, and suicide within the eating disorder population.

Foreword writer **Craig Johnson, PhD, CEDS, FAED,** is currently chief science officer at the Family Institute for Eating Recovery Center in Denver, CO, and clinical professor of psychiatry at University of Oklahoma College of Medicine. He has been a National Institute of Mental Health (NIMH)-funded researcher for over ten years and received distinguished contribution awards from the International Association of Eating Disorder Professionals (IAEDP), Academy for Eating Disorders (AED), National Eating Disorders Association (NEDA), National Association of Anorexia Nervosa and Associated Disorders (ANAD), and the American Red Cross. NEDA honored Johnson by creating the Craig Johnson Award for Clinical Excellence and Training, which is awarded annually.

FROM OUR PUBLISHER—

As the publisher at New Harbinger and a clinical psychologist since 1978, I know that emotional problems are best helped with evidence-based therapies. These are the treatments derived from scientific research (randomized controlled trials) that show what works. Whether these treatments are delivered by trained clinicians or found in a self-help book, they are designed to provide you with proven strategies to overcome your problem.

Therapies that aren't evidence-based—whether offered by clinicians or in books—are much less likely to help. In fact, therapies that aren't guided by science may not help you at all. That's why this New Harbinger book is based on scientific evidence that the treatment can relieve emotional pain.

This is important: if this book isn't enough, and you need the help of a skilled therapist, use the following resources to find a clinician trained in the evidence-based protocols appropriate for your problem. And if you need more support—a community that understands what you're going through and can show you ways to cope—resources for that are provided below, as well.

Real help is available for the problems you have been struggling with. The skills you can learn from evidence-based therapies will change your life.

Matthew McKay, PhD
Publisher, New Harbinger Publications

If you need a therapist, the following organization can help you find a therapist trained in cognitive behavioral therapy (CBT).

The Association for Behavioral & Cognitive Therapies (ABCT) Find-a-Therapist service offers a list of therapists schooled in CBT techniques. Therapists listed are licensed professionals who have met the membership requirements of ABCT and who have chosen to appear in the directory.
Please visit www.abct.org and click on *Find a Therapist*.

For additional support for patients, family, and friends, please contact the following:

National Eating Disorders Association (NEDA)
Visit www.nationaleatingdisorders.org

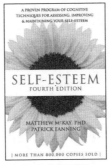

Register your **new harbinger** titles for additional benefits!

When you register your **new harbinger** title—purchased in any format, from any source—you get access to benefits like the following:

- Downloadable accessories like printable worksheets and extra content

- Instructional videos and audio files

- Information about updates, corrections, and new editions

Not every title has accessories, but we're adding new material all the time.

Access free accessories in 3 easy steps:

1. Sign in at NewHarbinger.com (or **register** to create an account).

2. Click on **register a book**. Search for your title and click the **register** button when it appears.

3. Click on the **book cover or title** to go to its details page. Click on **accessories** to view and access files.

That's all there is to it!

If you need help, visit:

NewHarbinger.com/accessories

new harbinger
CELEBRATING
40 YEARS